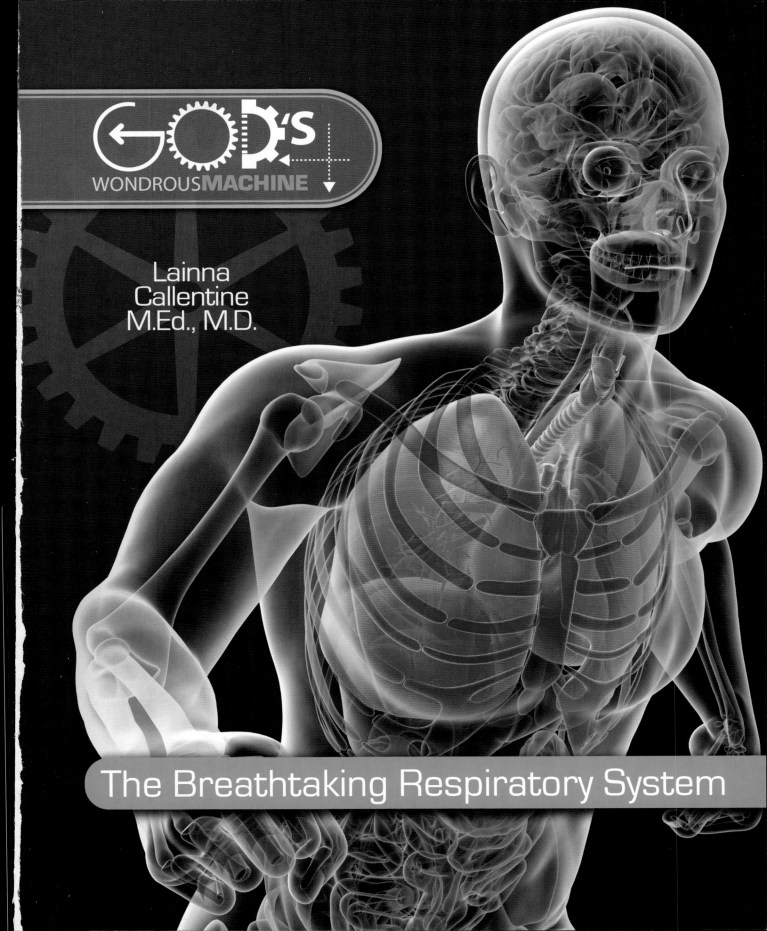

First printing: May 2015

Master Books®, P.O. Box 726,
Green Forest, AR 72638

Master Books® is a division of the
New Leaf Publishing Group, Inc.

ISBN: 978-0-89051-862-5
Library of Congress Number: 2015932194

Cover and Interior Design by Diana Bogardus

Unless otherwise noted, Scripture quotations are from the New International Version of the Bible.

Please consider requesting that a copy of this volume be purchased by your local library system.

Printed in China

Please visit our website for other great titles:
www.masterbooks.net

For information regarding author interviews, please contact the publicity department at
(870) 438-5288

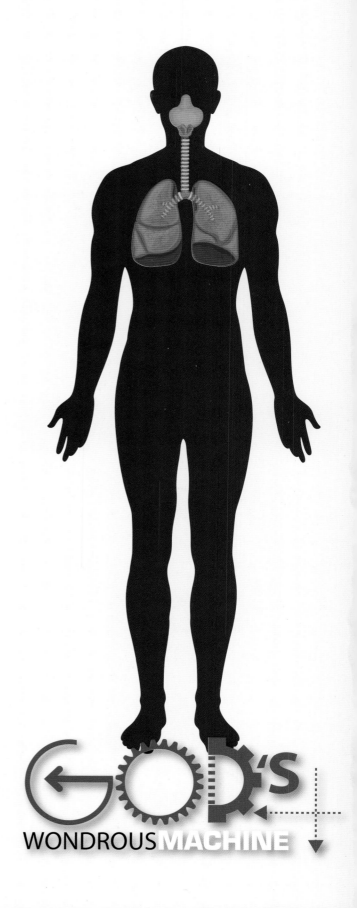

GOD'S
WONDROUS MACHINE

TABLE OF CONTENTS

How to Use This Book (All about Us!)

About this *God's Wondrous Machine* series:

Developed by a master's-trained teacher and homeschooling mother who happens to be a pediatrician, this is the second book in an innovative anatomy curriculum that focuses on the human body's respiratory system. It will create engaging opportunities for children to discover the wonders and workings of the human body.

Each book in this series delves into one of the major systems of the body; the first three of this nine-book series under development include the following:

 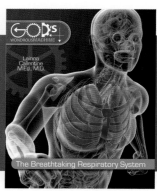 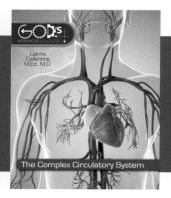

The book series will be bursting with vibrantly colorful images, interesting historical and weird facts, anatomy, physiology, and modern innovations. You will engage your senses and have a multitude of choices for hands-on exploration. You will discover aspects of the human body from a doctor's perspective. Each book will focus on a particular system of the body, discussing how it works and how it doesn't at times. Common questions kids ask are answered to stimulate curiosity, and your senses will be engaged as the world of medicine is demystified.

This series gives many perspectives in science education by connecting to other fields of study (i.e., history, sociology, psychology, and theology), and it encourages the reader to appreciate God's magnificent handiwork: your body.

God's Wondrous Machine series recognizes that every learner is not the same. Whether used in a homeschool or classroom setting, the series' hands-on activities are based on the educational theory of Multiple Intelligence by Howard Gardner (which states there are many types of intelligences and recognizes different learning styles: musical–rhythmic, visual–spatial, verbal–linguistic, logical–mathematical, bodily–kinesthetic, interpersonal, intrapersonal, and naturalistic). It is flexible enough for endless customization for the skills, interests, and abilities of each student.

Using the Curriculum Guide

This developing nine-book series will challenge the child in all facets of multiple intelligence. The parent/instructor is able to choose and customize hands-on activities that engage a multitude of learning styles and challenge the student to explore life's big issues. The program is specially designed for lower and upper elementary level students, including advanced learners with middle school proficiency!

You can use this book as an interesting:

▶ Unit Study

▶ Curriculum

▶ Supplemental Resource

An associated teacher guide is available. It contains perforated sheets for worksheets, and tests, in addition to a flexible educational calendar. This additional material allows for a multiple array of assessments for the instructor (i.e., project based, traditional testing, or portfolio assessment). It is designed to maximize the learning opportunities and retention of information from the book, as kids have fun learning about the mechanics and mysteries of themselves!

Did you know that your chest movement during respiration is not due to the air entering or leaving your lungs? This movement is due to your hardworking diaphragm. As the diaphragm contracts and moves downward, the space in your chest cavity increases in size. When you exhale, the opposite effect occurs.

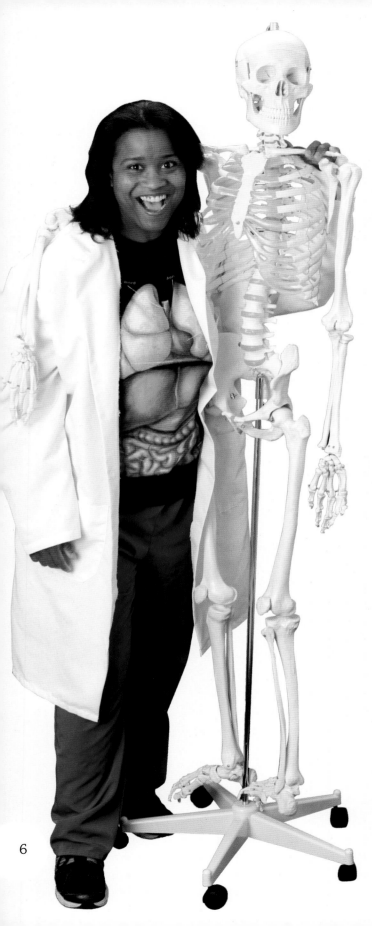

About the Author

Dr. Lainna Callentine has a passion for science. She spent many hours as a child turning over rocks and wading through streams chasing tadpoles. She is from a family of six children. Her parents grew up in the inner-city housing projects of Chicago, and her parents felt that education was a powerful tool. They instilled in her and her siblings a great love for learning.

Dr. Callentine wears many hats. She is a coach, teacher, pediatrician, and homeschool mother. She obtained her bachelor's degree in human development and social policy from Northwestern University in the school of education while competing as a full-scholarship athlete. She began her professional career as an elementary school teacher. She obtained her master's degree in education from Widener University. Then she went on to pursue her lifelong dream of becoming a doctor. Dr. Callentine obtained her medical degree from University of Illinois College of Medicine. She worked in one of the busiest emergency rooms in Illinois before answering the call to go home and homeschool her three children.

She founded Sciexperience and travels nationally as a speaker doing inspiring hands-on science workshops for all ages. She continues to utilize her medical training as a missionary doctor in a clinic for the uninsured in the suburbs of Chicago. She is a member of the Christian Medical and Dental Society and The Author's Guild. She enjoys basketball, time with her husband and three kids, and the outdoors.

Web information:

www.sciexperience.com

Facebook page: Sciexperience

LinkedIn: www.linkedin.com/pub/lainna-callentine-m-ed-m-d/50/744/a0b/

A Note from the Author

"Then the LORD God formed a man from the dust of the ground and breathed
into his nostrils the breath of life, and the man became a living being."
— Genesis 2:7

Why do we breathe? Why do we have to inhale and exhale, multiple times a minute without fail? Why don't we use gills or absorb oxygen through our skin as other animals do? It seems as if there are a number of other ways this could have been accomplished.

Breathing was designed for more than just the purpose of sustaining life, though it was certainly well designed for that. All creation was designed by God for a purpose, but not just a physical purpose. You were designed for a unique and special purpose. Breathing serves as a constant reminder of that first moment when God breathed into Adam and finished his creation. It is also a reminder of the nature of the Holy Spirit, often described as the Breath of God.

I continue to be amazed how creation declares the glory of God at every turn. The Breathtaking Respiratory System is no different. My prayer is that this will become evident to you with every new word and every weird or gross fact you learn. May your mind be open to discovering God's handiwork and recognizing the majesty that is reflected in the respiratory system. It will truly take your breath away.

In His Service,

Dr. Lainna Callentine

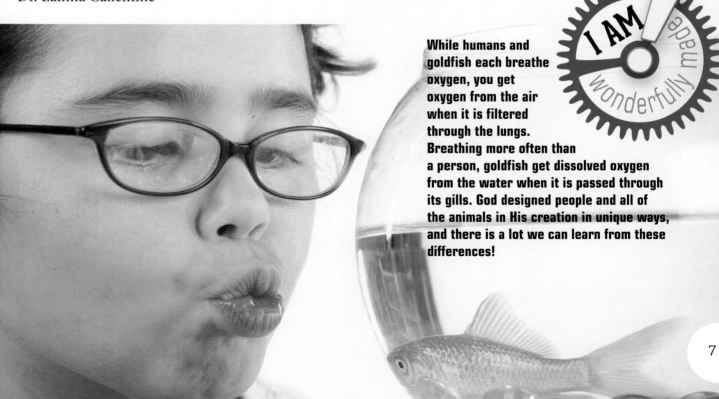

While humans and goldfish each breathe oxygen, you get oxygen from the air when it is filtered through the lungs. Breathing more often than a person, goldfish get dissolved oxygen from the water when it is passed through its gills. God designed people and all of the animals in His creation in unique ways, and there is a lot we can learn from these differences!

I AM wonderfully made

VOCABULARY LEVELS

Choose the word list based on your skill level. Every student should be able to master Level 1 words. Add words from Levels 2 and 3 as needed. More proficient students should be able to learn all three levels.

Level 1 Vocabulary

- Allergy
- Inhale
- Stethoscope
- Alveoli
- Larynx
- Upper Respiratory Tract
- Asthma
- Lower Respiratory Tract
- Virus
- Bacteria
- Mucus
- Vocal Cords
- Bronchi
- Nares
- Carbon Dioxide
- Pharynx
- Cilia
- Exhale

Level 2 Vocabulary

Review and Know Level 1 Vocabulary

- Allergens
- Influenza
- Trachea
- Anosmia
- Iron Lung
- Ventilation
- Antiseptic
- Laryngitis
- Bronchioles
- Pandemic
- Cystic Fibrosis
- Physiologist
- Diffusion
- Pleura Sac
- Epidemic
- Polio
- Epiglottis
- Sinuses

Level 3 Vocabulary

Review and Know Level 1 and 2 Vocabulary

- Apneustic Center
- Chemoreceptors
- Cribriform Plate
- Epithelium
- Gestation
- Goblet Cells
- Nasal Turbinate
- Organogenesis
- Pneumotaxic Center
- Surfactant
- Tracheostomy

The surface area of the lungs is roughly the same size as a tennis court. God's amazing design of the lungs means that you use this large surface area for the diffusion of oxygen and carbon dioxide for breathing!

See It, Say It, Know It!

Word [Pronunciation]	Definition
Allergens al·ler·gen (al´er-jen)	A foreign substance, such as mites in house dust or animal dander, that, when inhaled, causes the airways to narrow and produces symptoms of asthma
Allergy al·ler·gy (al´er-je)	An abnormally high, acquired sensitivity to certain substances, such as drugs, pollens, or microorganisms, that may include such symptoms as sneezing, itching, and skin rashes
Alveolus al-ve´o-lus Alveoli alve´oli (plural form)	Small air sacs or cavities in the lung that give the tissue a honey-comb appearance and expand its surface area for the exchange of oxygen and carbon dioxide
Anosmia an·os·mi·a	Loss of the sense of smell
Antiseptic an·ti·sep·tic	Capable of preventing infection by inhibiting the growth of bacteria
Apneustic Center app·new·stik sen·ter	The neurons in the brain stem controlling normal respiration
Asthma asth·ma	A common inflammatory disease of the lungs characterized by episodic airway obstruction caused by extensive narrowing of the bronchi and bronchioles. Common symptoms of asthma include wheezing, coughing, and shortness of breath.
Bacteria bac·te·ri·a	Organisms not able to be seen except under a microscope, found in rotting matter, in air, in soil, and in living bodies, some being the germs of disease
Bronchi bronc-i	The two branches of the trachea that extend into the lungs
Bronchioles bron·chi·ole	Any of the small, thin-walled tubes that branch from a bronchus and end in the alveolar sacs of the lung
Carbon Dioxide car·bon di·ox·ide	A colorless, odorless, incombustible gas, CO_2, formed during respiration, combustion, and organic decomposition and used in food refrigeration, carbonated beverages, inert atmospheres, fire extinguishers, and aerosols
Chemoreceptors che·mo·re·cep·tor	A sensory nerve stimulated by chemical means
Cilia cil·i·a	Short, hairlike, rhythmically beating organelles on the surface of certain cells that provide mobility, as in protozoans, or move fluids and particles along ducts in multicellular forms

9

Word [Pronunciation]	Definition
Cribriform Plate crib-i-form plate	Located in the ethmoid bone of the skull in the nasal cavity where the nerve endings of the sense of smell are found
Cystic Fibrosis cys'tic fibro'sis	An inherited disorder of the exocrine glands, usually developing during early childhood and affecting mainly the pancreas, respiratory system, and sweat glands. It is marked by the production of abnormally thick mucus by the affected glands, usually resulting in chronic respiratory infections and impaired pancreatic function.
Diffusion dif·fu·sion	The movement of atoms or molecules from an area of higher concentration to an area of lower concentration. Atoms and small molecules can move across a cell membrane by diffusion.
Epidemic ep·i·dem·ic	An outbreak of a disease or illness that spreads rapidly among individuals in an area or population at the same time
Epiglottis ep·i·glot·tis	The thin elastic cartilaginous structure located at the root of the tongue that folds over the glottis to prevent food and liquid from entering the trachea during the act of swallowing
Epithelium ep·i·the·li·um	Any tissue layer covering body surfaces or lining the internal surfaces of body cavities, tubes, and hollow organs
Exhale ex·hale	To breathe out
Gestation ges·ta·tion	The period during which unborn young are "carried" inside the womb
Goblet Cells Gob-let cells	Cells in the respiratory tract that produce mucus
Influenza in·flu·en·za	A highly contagious and often epidemic viral disease characterized by fever, tiredness, muscular aches and pains, and inflammation of the respiratory passages
Inhale in·hale	To breathe in; inspire
Iron Lung i'ron lung	An airtight metal cylinder enclosing the entire body up to the neck and providing artificial respiration when the respiratory muscles are paralyzed, as by poliomyelitis
Laryngitis lar·yn·gi·tis	Inflammation of the larynx, often with accompanying sore throat, hoarseness or loss of voice, and dry cough

10

Word [Pronunciation]	Definition
Larynx lar·ynx	The upper part of the trachea in most vertebrate animals, containing the vocal cords. The walls of the larynx are made of cartilage. Sound is produced by air passing through the larynx on the way to the lungs, causing the walls of the larynx to vibrate. The pitch of the sound that is produced can be altered by the pull of muscles, which changes the tension of the vocal cords. Also called voice box.
Lower Respiratory Tract lo·wer res·pir·a·tory tract	Consisting of all the structures in the respiratory tract lying below the larynx. The lower respiratory tract is composed of the trachea and lungs. The lungs include the bronchi, respiratory bronchioles, alveolar ducts, alveolar sacs, and alveoli.
Mucus mu·cus	The slimy, viscous substance secreted as a protective lubricant by mucous membranes. Mucus is composed chiefly of large glycoproteins called mucins and inorganic salts suspended in water.
Nares nar·is	An external opening in the nasal cavity of a vertebrate; a nostril
Nasal Turbinate Na·sal tur·bi·nate	Any of the scrolled spongy bones of the nasal passages in man and other vertebrates
Organogenesis or·gan·o·gen·e·sis	The development of bodily organs
Pandemic Pan·dem·ic	An epidemic that spreads over a very wide area, such as an entire country or continent
Pharynx phar·ynx	The passage that leads from the cavities of the nose and mouth to the larynx (voice box) and esophagus. Air passes through the pharynx on the way to the lungs, and food enters the esophagus from the pharynx.
Physiologist phys·i·ol·o·gist	Biologist specializing in physiology (the biological study of the functions of living organisms and their parts)
Pleura Sac pleu·ra sac	A membrane that encloses each lung and lines the chest cavity
Pneumotaxic Center pneu·mo·tax·ic sen·ter	A nerve center in the upper pons of the brain stem that rhythmically inhibits inspiration
Polio po·li·o	Poliomyelitis, an acute viral disease marked by inflammation of nerve cells of the brain stem and spinal cord that can affect the ability to walk and breathe

Word [Pronunciation]	Definition
Sinuses si·nus·es	A cavity or hollow space in a bone of the skull, especially one that connects with the nose
Stethoscope steth·o·scope	An instrument for listening to the sounds made within the body, typically consisting of a hollow disc that transmits the sound through hollow tubes to earpieces
Surfactant sur·fac·tant	Surfactant reduces the surface tension of fluid in the lungs and helps make the small air sacs in the lungs (alveoli) more stable.
Trachea tra·che·a	A thin-walled, cartilaginous tube descending from the larynx to the bronchi and carrying air to the lungs; also called windpipe
Tracheostomy tra·che·os·to·my	Surgical construction of an opening in the trachea, usually by making an incision in the front of the neck, for the insertion of a catheter or tube to facilitate breathing
Upper Respiratory Tract up·per res·puh·rah·tow·ree tract	Composed of the parts of the upper respiratory system: the nose, sinuses, pharynx, and larynx
Ventilation ven·ti·la·tion	The exchange of air between the lungs and the environment, including inhalation and exhalation
Virus vi·rus	Any of various extremely small, often disease-causing agents consisting of a particle (the virion), containing a segment of RNA or DNA within a protein coat known as a capsid. Viruses are not technically considered living organisms because they cannot carry out biological processes.
Vocal Cords vo'·cal cords	The two folded pairs of membranes in the larynx (voice box) that vibrate when air that is exhaled passes through them, producing sound

*Most pronunciation keys from: http://medical-dictionary.thefreedictionary.com

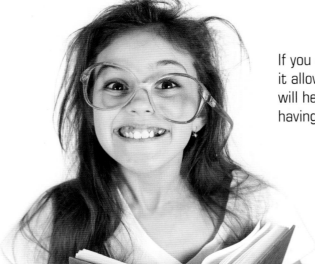

If you sit up straight while reading a book out loud, it allows you to use more of your lung capacity. This will help keep you from getting short of breath or having to gasp for air in the middle of a sentence!

When you laugh, the muscles in your chest and your diaphragm contract, pushing air out of the lungs in a quick rush that makes your larynx vibrate to make the sound of laughter – ha ha! It has been observed that the average young child laughs nearly 300 times in a day. Adults, on average, laugh 15 to 100 times a day.

Laughter is good medicine! It helps to reduce pain and blood sugar levels. Proverbs 17:22 says, "A cheerful heart is good medicine, but a crushed spirit dries up the bones."

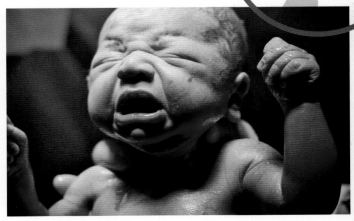

With a loud-piercing wail, each of us entered this world as a crying baby taking in our first breath of air. That breath ushers in a new independent life outside the mother's womb. Created from the dust on the ground and with the breath God breathed into his lungs, Adam took his first breath. This life-giving force originates from none other than God: the giver of life and breath. The respiratory system is yet another demonstration of God's provision, our human frailty, and our complete dependence on Him.

Why do we breathe? We breathe because we eat. Okay, that sounds a bit ridiculous. But it makes sense when we look at our bodies as an incredible engine. For an engine to carry out all of its processes, it needs energy. Oxygen is needed to burn and utilize the fuel we eat. The billions of cells in our bodies grab the oxygen we breathe from the red blood cells that travel by and utilize it to perform all of its complicated actions. The cells throw out the garbage from their day's work in the form of a gas called carbon dioxide. The lungs inhale oxygen and exhale carbon dioxide.

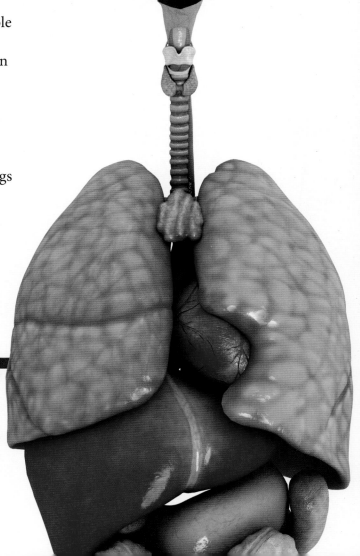

on the nose.

The capillaries in the lungs would extend 1,600 kilometers, almost 995 miles, if placed end to end. That is just slightly shorter than the distance between New York City and Tampa, Florida or almost equal to the distance between Chicago and Denver.

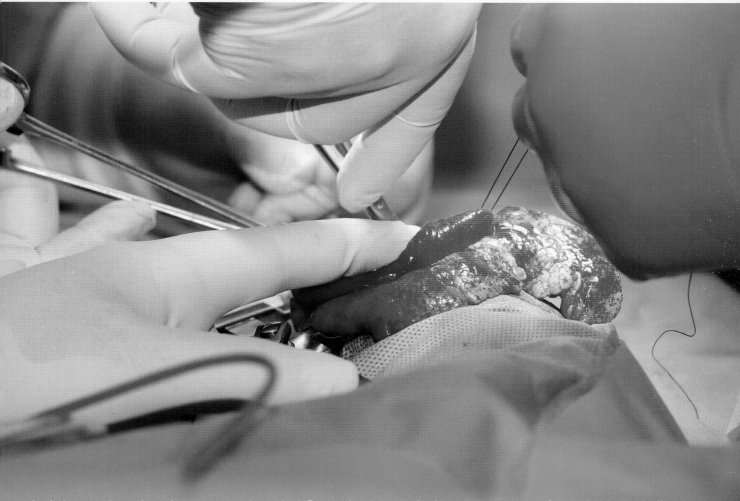

Isn't it amazing what doctors can do today! Surgeries to repair damage to parts of your body, including those of an infant's lung like this one, can now be done safely.

Sit back and breathe in. Come, as we embark on a captivating voyage through the wind tunnels of the body, and be prepared to be amazed. At the first stop on our journey, we will peer into the Bible and see what God's Word says about this life force. We will then take a look back in the pages of time and learn about discoveries that have helped shape our understanding of the respiratory system today. We will learn about the anatomy and physiology of this inverted tree-like structure called the lungs.

Discover remarkable things about your soft, spongy lungs. Did you know it is the only organ in your body that can actually float on water? The surface area of the alveoli (the small air sacs of the lungs) alone could cover the surface of an entire tennis court! Breeze in and witness this incredible expanse of God's Wondrous Machine. It will take your breath away!

15

But isn't history just about a bunch of dead people? Why should it matter to me? How important is medical history for a particular system of the body? The dates and events are meaningless to our lives, right? Wrong. As you dive into "God's Wondrous Machine," you will see how these events have shaped what we understand to be true today. We encounter real problems in life. It is through those problems that we acquire new knowledge and original ways to solve those problems. History connects the past with the present and the future. When we study history, we can observe how things change over time and understand the situations and life circumstances that generate the necessity of innovation and invention. As you read, observe the frailty of our being and how God has given us each unique minds to help impact the world in which we live. You will see that the knowledge base that you now bring to the table far exceeds the knowledge of people from yesterday. We are confronted with new problems. The hope is that you will play a part in creating real solutions to the problems we encounter today to impact the advances of tomorrow.

Let's set sail through the pages of time and see how the various discoveries have provided a platform for future breakthroughs.

500 B.C.
Anaximenes, of ancient Greece, believed that all things were made of air. He called it *pneuma* which means "breath" in Greek. The Greeks believed everything was alive and breathing.

470 B.C.
Empedocles, the Greek philosopher, taught that all things were made of four elements — earth, air, fire, and water.

350 B.C.
Aristotle thought the heart was on fire. Breathing in cooled the fire and kept it from burning up the whole body.

1660
Marcello Malpighi, born in Crevalcore, Italy, March 10, 1628, showed that the lungs consist of many small air pockets and a complex system of blood vessels by observing capillaries through a microscope. He described the circulation of blood.

1765
John Morgan founded the first medical school in America at the College of Pennsylvania.

1772-1774
Joseph Priestley discovered nitrous oxide and is credited with the discovery of oxygen.

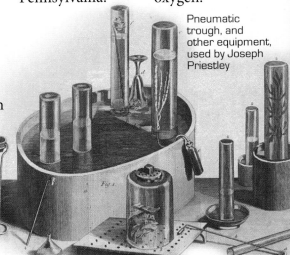

Pneumatic trough, and other equipment, used by Joseph Priestley

16

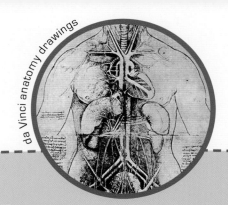
da Vinci anatomy drawings

280-271 B.C.
Greek physician Erasistratus came very close to recognizing the circulation of the blood, especially by noting the relationship of the lungs to the circulating system.

A.D. 170
Galen taught that the secret of life was a spirit or *pneuma* that came from the air.

1500
Leonardo da Vinci, Italian painter and inventor, suggested that air was not made from one element but a combination of two gases.

1643
Evangelista Torricelli proved that air had weight and took up space.

1660
Robert Hooke, an Englishman, found that parts of the body act like pumps. Our ribs help pump air in and out of the lungs.

Re-enactment of the first operation under anesthesia

1779
Thomas Beddoes and Humphry Davy recognized nitrous oxide's anesthetizing effects, but did not think to use it to take away pain.

1779
Lavoisier proposed the name "oxygen" for the part of air that is breathed and responsible for combustion. He discovered that air was composed mainly of two components — oxygen and nitrogen.

1819
Treatise on Diagnosis by Listening to Sounds by physician Theophile René Laennec was written in which he demonstrated the use of a tube for investigating the lungs and heart sounds.

1845
Anesthetic inhaler invented. *Anesthetic* comes from the Greek word meaning "loss of feeling." Prior to the invention of anesthesia, patients were strapped down and held by strong individuals as the surgeon speedily worked.

1845
William Morton, an American doctor, used ether to extract a tooth from a patient. A sealed glass jar with an air valve containing several ether-soaked sponges was used, with a long rubber tube as a mouthpiece.

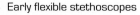
Early flexible stethoscopes

Jules Bordet

1847

Chloroform came into use. It was found that it was particularly useful in childbirth by James Young Simpson. This met a great deal of criticism — it was believed that it was always a woman's fate to suffer pain during childbirth. Queen Victoria popularized its use when she used it during the birth of her seventh child, Leopold.

1855

George Phillip Cammann, an American doctor, took Laennec's idea and developed the stethoscope we know today.

1882

Robert Koch discovers the bacterium that causes tuberculosis, the first definite association of a germ with a specific human disease.

1904

The National Association for the Study and Prevention of Tuberculosis was founded. This organization later became the American Lung Association.

1906

Jules Bordet discovered *Bordetella pertussis*, the bacterium that causes whooping cough.

Dr. Dorothy Andersen

Queen Victoria, with the Princess Royal

1938

Dr. Dorothy Andersen, a pathologist at Columbia-Presbyterian Babies and Children's Hospital in New York, was the first to document and observe the problems of cystic fibrosis, a genetic disease.

1953

Dr. Paul di Sant'Agnese developed an effective technique of diagnosing cystic fibrosis called the Sweat Test.

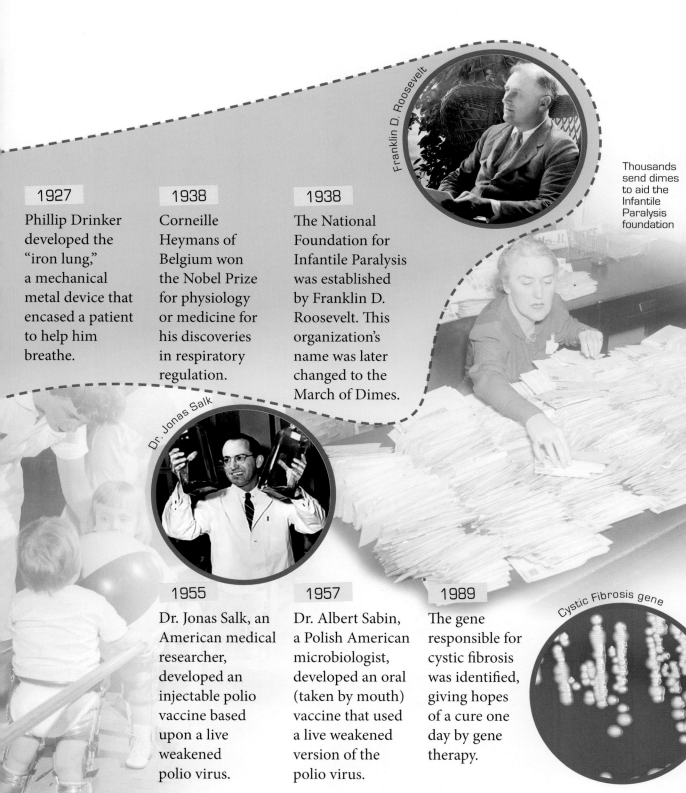

1927

Phillip Drinker developed the "iron lung," a mechanical metal device that encased a patient to help him breathe.

1938

Corneille Heymans of Belgium won the Nobel Prize for physiology or medicine for his discoveries in respiratory regulation.

1938

The National Foundation for Infantile Paralysis was established by Franklin D. Roosevelt. This organization's name was later changed to the March of Dimes.

Franklin D. Roosevelt

Thousands send dimes to aid the Infantile Paralysis foundation

Dr. Jonas Salk

1955

Dr. Jonas Salk, an American medical researcher, developed an injectable polio vaccine based upon a live weakened polio virus.

1957

Dr. Albert Sabin, a Polish American microbiologist, developed an oral (taken by mouth) vaccine that used a live weakened version of the polio virus.

1989

The gene responsible for cystic fibrosis was identified, giving hopes of a cure one day by gene therapy.

Cystic Fibrosis gene

19

Joseph Priestley: The Dissenter Discovers Oxygen

Joseph Priestley (1733–1804) was born on March 13, 1733, in Fieldhead, England. Joseph's father died shortly after his birth. Joseph's mother was a devout religious woman who taught Joseph about God. As Joseph grew, he had a ravenous appetite for the Bible and learning. Faith and religion were central parts of daily life in England. England's official church was the Anglican Church, or the Church of England. It was a powerful organization and controlled many aspects of daily life. As Joseph matured in his faith, his views changed from the views held by the Anglican Church. Joseph became a dissenter. Dissenters were a diverse group that included Baptists, Lutherans, Methodists, Presbyterians, and Quakers that disagreed with the Church of England and broke away. Dissenters had limited rights in England. They could not attend the large universities, like Oxford and Cambridge. Nonetheless, Joseph pursued his passion for learning and God. He became an instructor at a local academy, a scientist, and was ordained as a Dissenting minister.

Priestley published six volumes of *Experiments and Observations on Different Kinds of Air* between 1772 and 1790. He detailed his experiments on gases or "airs." He is credited for the discovery of several gases: nitrogen dioxide, ammonia, nitrous oxide (laughing gas), nitrogen, and oxygen. The success that Priestley experienced as a scientist is credited to his keen mind and his ability to design ingenious contraptions to study gases he discovered.

The Breath of Life

Breathing is essential to life. Without the air that rushes into your lungs you would cease to exist. The Bible makes many references to breathing. Our Heavenly Father is the giver of life and through His breath He calls all creatures into existence. In Genesis 2:7 it says, "Then the Lord God formed a man from the dust of the ground and breathed into his nostrils the breath of life, and the man became a living being."

There is no evidence here of man being formed from an evolutionary process, but rather being formed from the actual loving hands of God. Job, through all his adversity, knew where his life force came from. In Job 33:4 he states, "The Spirit of God has made me; the breath of the Almighty gives me life." Remember, as Psalm 150:6 states, "Let everything that has breath praise the Lord. Praise the Lord."

Biblical References:			
2 Samuel 22:16	Job 4:9	John 20:22	Acts 17:25
Isaiah 11:4	Ezekiel 37:5–10	Isaiah 30:28	

I AM wonderfully made

The Haldanes and Their Bad Gas

Today, scientific research is heavily managed and monitored. In the 1970s, the Food and Drug Administration (FDA) developed laws to protect human subjects taking part in clinical trials. Clinical trials are research studies that determine how well new medical approaches work in people.

Prior to this time, there was no standard on how things were tested on people. Many doctors and scientists would do unsafe practices on themselves or others in order to observe and learn new medical advances. There are two such scientists, father and son, who used themselves as human guinea pigs. (Guinea pigs have been commonly used in laboratory studies.) John and Jack Haldane utilized their bodies for scientific exploration. They made many contributions to our understanding of the respiratory system and the nature of gases.

John Haldane was a Scottish physiologist born in the late 1800s. A physiologist is a type of scientist that strives to understand how body systems work. Mr. Haldane demonstrated an insatiable thirst for knowledge. He would conduct experiments on himself. He would check the quality of air by locking himself in closed chambers and inhaling potentially deadly gases. He would then record the effects it had on his body and mind. John's son, Jack, was quick to get into the act. Jack began his own experimentation at three years of age when he gladly allowed his father to take a small amount of his blood for study. At the ripe old age of four years, Jack started breathing "bad air" in the underground railway and mines, and at 13 years he dove into the ocean in

a leaky diving suit. Jack was a child scientist by his father's side.

On many occasions, the Haldanes felt the ill effects of their experiments. They suffered from headaches, vomiting, passing out, and on some occasions even turned blue. John was able to show that most of these ill effects were not due to a lack of oxygen but a build-up of carbon dioxide in their bloodstream.

They did many crazy things. It is not surprising that the family motto of the Haldane family was just one word — "suffer." They inhaled many mixtures of gases and studied the effects on their bodies. They were one of the first to identify that breathing was controlled by the blood-brain barrier that transported gases to a sensitive area of the brain. They were the experts on the hazards of breathing bad air. Their discoveries revolutionized and protected the jobs of miners, soldiers, deep sea divers, and submarine dwellers. They unlocked the mysteries of respiration and the gases that affect us.

John Haldane came up with the idea of using canaries as an early warning system. The miners carried a caged canary into the coal mine and if dangerous gases like carbon monoxide were present they would kill the canary before the miners felt the ill effects.

The breathtaking respiratory system can be divided into two general parts: the upper respiratory tract and the lower respiratory tract. The upper respiratory tract is more like a tunnel system that propels the air downward. The air cannot be used by the lungs until it arrives at the lower respiratory tract.

If the actual spongy tissues of the lungs were removed and the respiratory tunnels were left, it would resemble an upside-down tree. The respiratory tree originates at the trachea (the trunk) and spreads, dividing to smaller and smaller branches called the bronchioles. Let's take a closer look at the different parts, starting with the upper respiratory tract.

Upper Respiratory Tract

The main function of the upper respiratory tract, is to be the passageway for air to the lungs. The air rushes in and is propelled down the tract. From top to bottom, the parts of the upper respiratory tract are as follows:

1. Nose

2. Sinuses

3. Pharynx

4. Larynx

Your nose is really cool! At the top of the nasal cavity there is a space the size of a postage stamp that has some 10 million small receptor cells. Your nose doesn't only just help you breathe and smell stuff; it's also connected to your sense of taste. That's why it's hard to taste your food when you have a stopped-up nose!

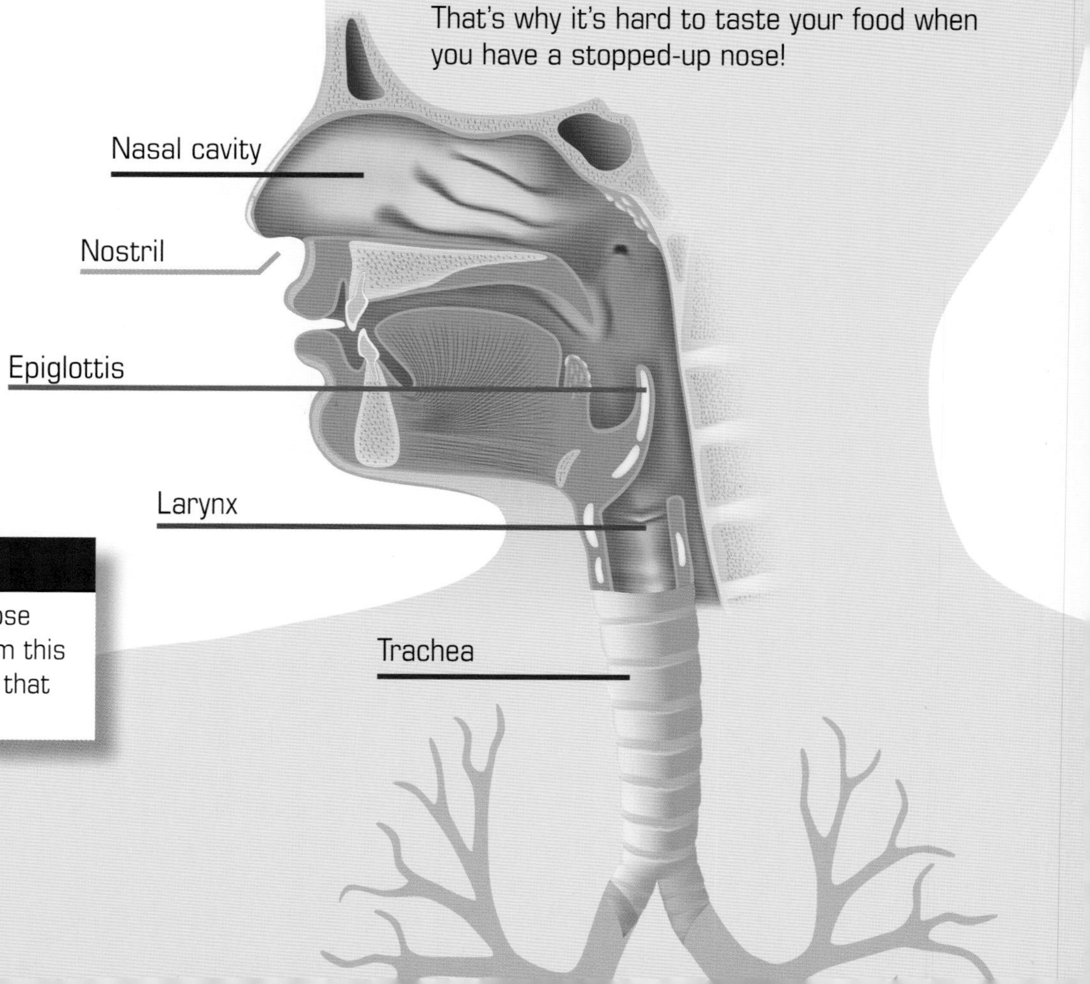

Nasal cavity

Nostril

Epiglottis

Larynx

Trachea

Word Wise!

NOSTHYRL means "nose hole" in old English. From this came the word "nostril" that we know today!

22

Mucus: A Bat in the Cave

A bat in the cave, snot, phlegm, and loogie are just a few terms people use when referring to the wonderful substance of mucus. Before starting our downward journey through the tract, let's take a look at this natural multipurpose lubricant called mucus. Most people find the discussion of mucus a bit gross. It is actually a wonderful invention by our Heavenly Father. What is that? You say that it has never been part of your prayers when thanking God for His many provisions? There are so many things we take for granted in our bodies until they malfunction. Step up as we take an appreciative look at mucus.

Mucus is a lubricant. A lubricant is something that is slimy and cuts down friction on surfaces as things slide past. It has many functions aside from just being slimy. Mucus can be as thick and sticky as maple syrup. This stickiness allows it to trap bits and pieces of dust and dirt. In addition, it traps unwanted visitors into our bodies like nasty, germy bacteria. Mucus keeps things nice and moist, preventing the lining of our nose, stomach, and intestines from drying out. It also has antiseptic enzymes within its goo. These antiseptic enzymes act on bacteria and decrease the incidence of infections. The mucus traps these particles and other poten- tially harmful substances and whisks them off to the pharynx to be swallowed and demolished by digestive juices in the stomach.

Eeeewwwww!

Way back in the Middle Ages, it was believed the body was composed of four humors, or fluids. Phlegm, or mucus, was one of these mistaken humors. If a person's body was off balance and not well, the fault was attributed to one of the humors. If you felt sluggish and emotionally up and down, this was most likely due to being "phlegmatic." In other words, too much phlegm or mucus within your body was upsetting your healthy balance.

There are cells in your body called goblet cells that make this hard-working substance of mucus. Mucus is composed of mucopolysaccharides (mew-kow-pol-ee-sack-ah-rides). The recipe for mucus is 95% water, 2% mucin, and 2–3% salt. The mucin gives the mucus its slimy goodness and sticky composition. The average person produces about one quart of mucus a day! A quart is the size of the container in which milk, mayo, and motor oil are usually purchased.

Sometimes when your nose starts to itch on the inside, you have an overwhelming urge to sneeze. In one sneeze, thousands of tiny droplets of snot and other bacteria hitchhikers sail out of your nose like a rocket into the air space surrounding you. Anyone within three to five feet may be pelted by the aerosol. There has been long debate about how fast a snot rocket can be ejected. Some have stated that it can hit speeds up to 100 miles an hour. In the show *Mythbusters*, Jamie Hyneman and Adam Savage set up high-speed cameras to be eyewitnesses to the physics of mucoid propulsion. They sniffed items that would cause forceful sneezing. Taking turns as great scientists, they recorded their results. Adam clocked a speed of 35 mph and Jamie rocketed at 39 mph.

The average person produces about one quart of snot a day!

on the nose.

23

The Nose

The nose is one of the top producers of mucus. The nose's function is to warm and filter the air. It is the passageway for air where it is humidified (water is added to it) and moistened. Inside your nose, there are thousands of hairs. These hairs partner with the mucus to provide a trap for dust. Once tickled, the hairs can trigger a sneeze to expel any unwanted items.

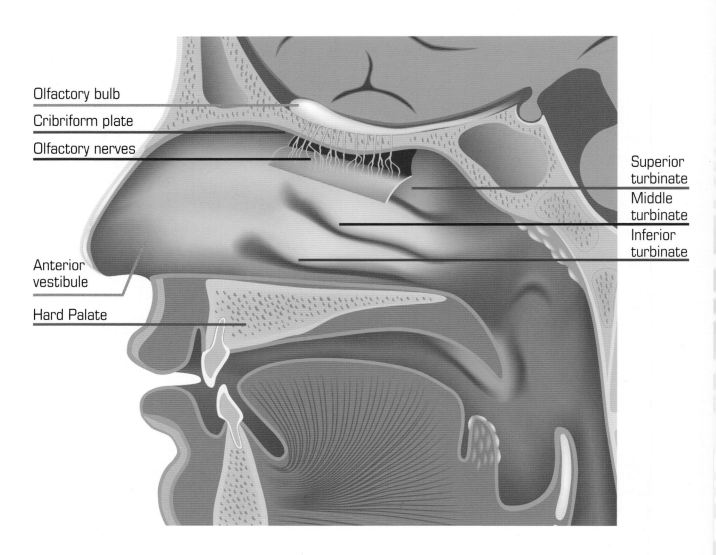

Parts of the Nose

Air enters the nose at the nares. These two openings enter at the anterior vestibule. The anterior vestibule is the area in which most nose bleeds occur. Many kids and adults alike may from time to time engage in attempts to extract a hardened mucoid fragment from their nose — a booger. The nose has many blood vessels that are close to the lining on the inside. It is through

God gave us an incredible ability to smell. We can enjoy the fragrances of flowers, good food, and even the rain as it falls. Most people can distinguish over 10,000 different odors, and women have a better sense of smell than men. Dogs are still better at smelling than we are! They can detect the tiniest traces of an odor and can even smell the chemicals that come with emotions like fear or sadness.

these vessels that warm blood flows, assisting in warming the air that you inhale. A scrape in this area can cause a nosebleed. The art of nose picking is greatly frowned upon in modern-day society. In the 1500s, it was considered acceptable behavior. There was even a code of etiquette on how to pick your nose while in the company of others.

Next in line is the nasal turbinate or concha. There are three bony plates on each side of the nose, covered with the nasal lining. These nooks and crannies serve to increase the surface area of the nasal cavity and cause the air to be more turbulent in flow. This turbulence and surface area further aids the nose to filter, cleanse, warm, and moisten the air you breathe. The right and the left sides of your nasal cavity are divided by the septum.

The cribriform plate lies at the top of the nasal cavity. It is the part of the skull that separates the brain from the nasal cavity. There is a special nerve network that emerges at this site. The olfactory bulb sends nerve endings through openings in this region. Olfactory nerves deal with our sense of smell. A skull fracture in this area can potentially damage these nerves and cause anosmia (an-OHZ-me-uh), a loss of the ability to smell.

We take our sense of smell for granted. Your sense of smell helps you to taste foods. It helps you to smell the light fragrance of a rose. Most importantly, it helps you to sense smells that could be dangerous to you like the smell of rancid milk. You smell the milk and know instantly it is something you do not want to drink.

Animals like bloodhound dogs have an exquisite sense of smell. Bloodhounds have approximately 230 million olfactory cells! That is 40 times greater than we humans have. It is amazing to watch these dogs happily at work. Bloodhounds can sniff an article of clothing and obtain the unique odor of a person. This smell sticks to the dog's scent receptors in its nose. The odor serves like a smell photograph of the person to the dog. The dog's instincts take over and it can track the scent of an individual for miles.

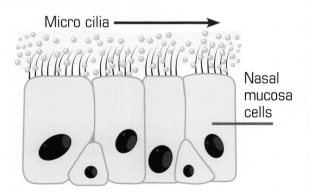

Micro cilia

Nasal mucosa cells

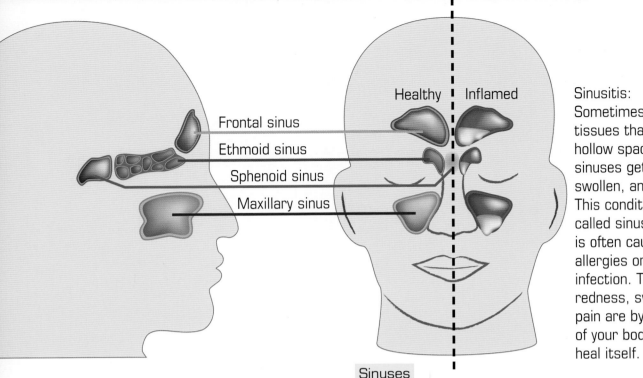

Frontal sinus
Ethmoid sinus
Sphenoid sinus
Maxillary sinus

Healthy | Inflamed

Sinusitis: Sometimes the tissues that line the hollow spaces of the sinuses get red, swollen, and painful. This condition is called sinusitis, and is often caused by allergies or an infection. The redness, swelling and pain are by-products of your body trying to heal itself.

Sinuses

Within the confines of your facial bones lie four pairs of hollow spaces. These spaces are called the sinuses. The names of the four pairs are (1) frontal, (2) sphenoid, (3) ethmoid, and (4) maxillary.

Their function is to assist in warming and moistening the air that you inhale. It provides a hollow space that acts like a resonance chamber for speech production. A resonance chamber is a completely enclosed space aside one hole that allows sound to enter. Sound waves enter through the hole and are amplified (made louder). For example, in stringed instruments like the guitar or violin, the hollow body is this type of chamber. The sound hole lies below the strings. As the strings are strummed they vibrate, causing sound.

Have you ever noticed when you have a cold with an extremely "stuffy" nose that the sound of your voice is very different? Many people state that their voice sounds "nasal" when they have a cold. This happens when this one hole that opens into each of the sinuses becomes swollen or plugged off. Sounds cannot resonate as well and the characteristic "nasal" voice quality is heard.

The hollow sinuses allow the skull to weigh less. They also produce mucus to trap and get rid of unwanted materials that enter. The mucus in the sinuses drains through their hole into the nasal cavity. In the nasal cavity, there are nasal hairs near the entrance of the nose. Germ droplets that aren't caught in the nose hairs may enter the sinuses. The sinuses will become irritated and swollen. This swelling will block off the drainage of the sinuses. The sinuses become a closed container of mucus and germy critters. The space becomes like a stagnant pool. These germs love warm, dark, and moist environments. There they grow, multiply, and have a party. The result is a sinus infection or sinusitis. (*Sinu:* hollow cavity, *-itis:* inflammation.) The face or forehead over the infected area of the sinus can become swollen and red.

Word Wise!

"RHINITIS" is what we doctors call inflamed (swollen) nasal membranes. It's commonly known as having a stuffy or runny nose!

Your sinuses aren't fully developed after birth. The frontal sinuses and sphenoid sinuses don't begin to develop until a child reaches his or her second birthday. The actual cavities cannot be seen by x-ray imaging until the child is at least five or six years old. Your sinuses continue to grow until your teenage years.

Stages of sinus development

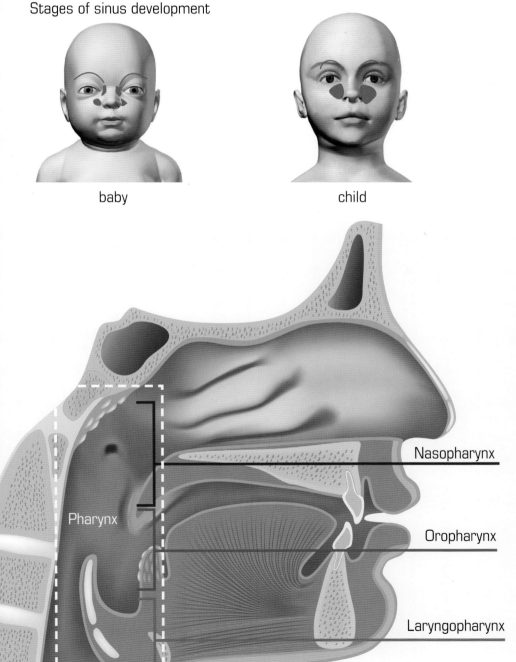

baby

child

teenager

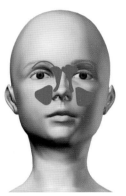

Pharynx

Air enters the nose and travels down to the pharynx. The pharynx is the back of your throat. Your oral cavity, the inside of your mouth, and your nasal cavity both open up in the back to join together at the pharynx. The area directly behind the nasal cavity is called the nasopharynx. The area directly behind your oral cavity is called the oropharynx. See the pattern? We use very specific terms in Anatomy in order to effectively communicate with precision.

Pharynx

Nasopharynx

Oropharynx

Laryngopharynx

27

The Larynx

The pharynx meets up with the larynx. The area where the pharynx and larynx meet is called the laryngopharynx. (The larynx can be considered part of the upper or lower respiratory tract.) This whole anatomy thing is a piece of cake, right? The larynx is the home of your vocal cords. The vocal cords are like the reed of a wind instrument. When air goes by them they vibrate and produce sound. Kids' voices are much different from adult voices. In males, at puberty, the larynx and vocal cords grow larger. The vocal cords also become longer and thicker. These changes are what cause a man's voice to deepen. Speaking of vocal cords, during Roman times, it was not uncommon for a master to give his slave a tea made from dieffenbachia (dumb plant). The slave was forced to drink the tea. The tea caused the slave's tongue and mouth to swell. It even paralyzed the slave's throat. This was given to the slave prior to going to the market to ensure he or she was unable to speak and gossip about their master's household. As you can image, if too much was given, the swelling would cut off the airways and could lead to death.

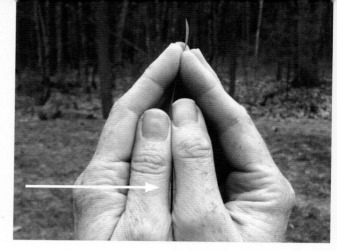

In the summer, it is fun to take a blade of grass, stretch it taut, grasp it tightly between your thumbs, and blow forcefully. A loud whistling noise can be heard as the blade of grass vibrates in the rushing air much like your vocal cords.

The outside of the throat is a prominent area commonly called the Adam's apple. This area is more noticeable in men than women. The Adam's apple does not enlarge in males until puberty as their cartilage, muscles, and vocal cords in the larynx enlarge. Since this enlargement normally occurs in males, this term originates from the account of Adam and Eve in Genesis. Adam was offered the forbidden fruit from Eve. The debate about the type of fruit has been questioned. In folk tales, it is said that part of the apple got stuck in Adam's throat and continues to be a reminder of his original sin.

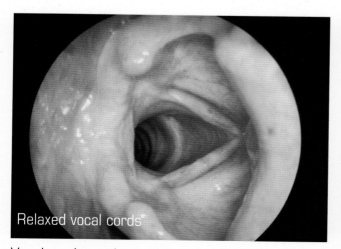

Relaxed vocal cords

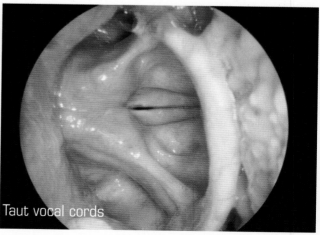

Taut vocal cords

Vocal cords are located in the larynx, part of the neck. When taut or tight, they produce sound as air from the lungs is passed through them. This is used to form sounds such as singing and speech.

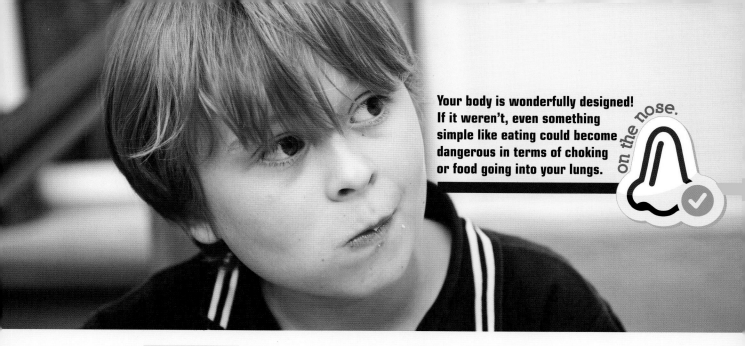

The Epiglottis

The larynx is the end of the line for the upper respiratory tract. It is at this point that you arrive at a fork in the road. The tunnel system splits. One part runs down to the lungs and the other part runs to the esophagus. The esophagus is the food tube that transports what you eat to your stomach. Your air and your food share the passage until arriving at this fork in the road. God has designed an ingenious and effective mechanism to prevent food from entering your lungs. He has designed the "lid." Well, it isn't really named the "lid." It is called the epiglottis. It is a little piece of cartilage that acts as a lid, covering the trachea and larynx when we eat and drink. It prevents us from choking when we swallow. Sometimes you can see the top of the epiglottis when you ask someone to stick out their tongue and say "ah."

You may have heard someone tell you, "Don't talk with your mouth full." Your body was not designed to breathe and swallow at the same time. In order to talk or laugh, air has to rush in and out of your lungs. The epiglottis remains open when you talk and laugh. When you swallow food, the epiglottis slams down like a lid to keep food stuff from entering your lungs. The epiglottis doesn't shut when you are eating and laughing at the same time. This may lead to food going down your "windpipe." This is called "aspiration" and leads to choking.

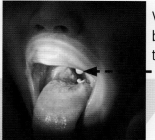

Visible epiglottis at the back of the throat on a two year old.

Epiglottis

The lower respiratory tract is composed of the trachea and lungs. The lungs include the bronchi, respiratory bronchioles, alveolar ducts, alveolar sacs, and alveoli. Wow! That is a mouthful. No worries. Let's walk by each, one by one. The lower respiratory system is where the business of breathing occurs. The trachea and the bronchi act as a passageway for air to the lungs. The lungs are the site for exchange of gases. They allow us to breathe. Just a quick point: the word alveolus is used when you are talking about a single one of these grape-like structures. The word alveoli is used when you are referring to many of these grape-like structures. It is the plural form.

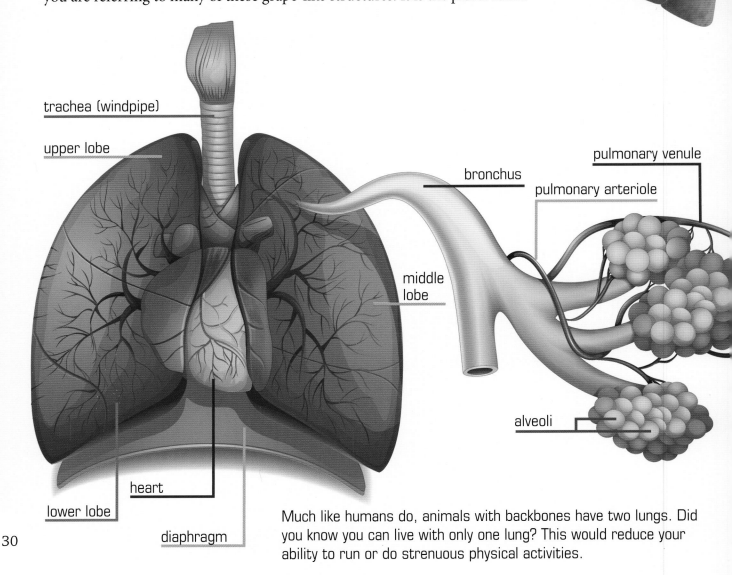

trachea (windpipe)

upper lobe

pulmonary venule

bronchus

pulmonary arteriole

middle lobe

alveoli

heart

lower lobe

diaphragm

Much like humans do, animals with backbones have two lungs. Did you know you can live with only one lung? This would reduce your ability to run or do strenuous physical activities.

The Trachea

The trachea brings air into the lungs. It has many C-shaped flexible cartilage rings that run down its length. The structure of the trachea resembles the flexible aluminum or plastic tubing that is found on the back of your laundry dryer. These C-shaped cartilage rings help to keep the trachea from collapsing. The rings do not run completely around the trachea. Why do you think God designed it that way? Remember when we talked about that "fork in the road"? What structure runs directly behind the trachea? Bingo! The esophagus! If the trachea's rings ran completely around, when you swallowed food it would bounce through like a car on rumble strips on a highway.

Sometimes due to illness or a birth defect, a person may have problems maintaining an open airway in order to breathe. A tracheostomy may be used to help keep a person's airway open and make it easier to breathe. This procedure is indicated in cases where a person does not have a cough reflex. The cough reflex is normally triggered when something irritates the respiratory tract and causes one to cough. This reflex protects the airway. A tube is inserted below the vocal cords and allows them to breathe easier.

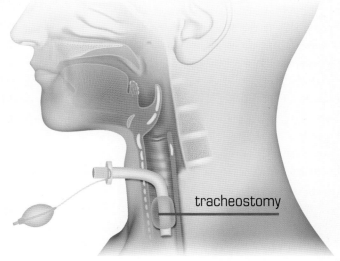

tracheostomy

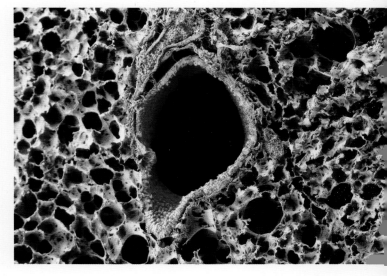

Lung tissue

The Lungs

The lungs are spongy organs. They are composed of many passageways and microscopic air sacs. The lungs are encased in the pleura sac. This sac has two layers. It allows the lungs to expand and recoil without causing friction or rubbing on the ribs.

There are two lungs, the right and left. The right lung has three segments and the left lung has two segments. The left lung has one segment less due to the space that is occupied by the heart.

The trachea enters the lungs and divides into two tunnels, the right and left bronchus. The bronchus divides into smaller and smaller branches as the travel deeper into the lungs. The bronchi enter the lungs and branch into smaller secondary (second) and tertiary (third) bronchi, respectively. The tertiary bronchi divide into ever-smaller branches called the bronchioles. The tunnels become smaller and smaller. At the end of the bronchioles is a cluster of air sacs known as alveoli. These alveoli are grouped together like clusters of grapes. This is where carbon dioxide (CO_2) is traded for oxygen. Oxygen is needed for our body to perform all of its duties. We will look more at this momentarily.

31

Cilia

Cilia are hair-like projections that line the larger airways of the lungs. These hairs beat together in a coordinated motion that causes a current of mucus that is swept to the back of the throat to be coughed out or swallowed. The mucus in the lungs is produced by a special cell called the goblet cell. The mucus lies on the top layer over the cilia. Cigarette smoking is harmful to the cilia. If the cilia are unable to move, then mucus builds up in the airways.

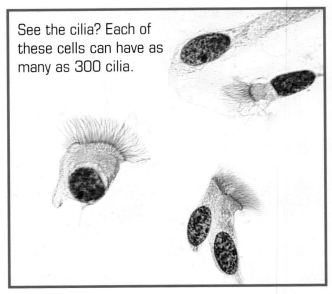

See the cilia? Each of these cells can have as many as 300 cilia.

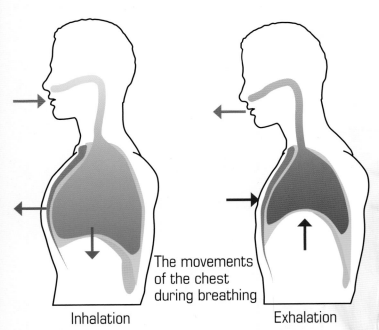

The movements of the chest during breathing

Inhalation

Exhalation

The diaphragm is a large sheet-like muscle that your lungs rest on. The diaphragm separates the thorax, the chest cavity, from the abdominal cavity. When you take a breath in, the diaphragm contracts and moves downward as your lungs expand. In exhalation, the diaphragm moves back up, expelling the air from your lungs.

Three other structures outside the lungs play an important role in breathing. Those three structures are the ribs, the intercostal muscles, and the diaphragm. The ribs surround your chest cavity. They attach in the back to your spine. In the front, most attach to the sternum, except for the last couple of ribs. The ribs function like the handle of a bucket. During inhalation your ribs are lifted up and out by the intercostal muscles, and during exhalation they move down and in.

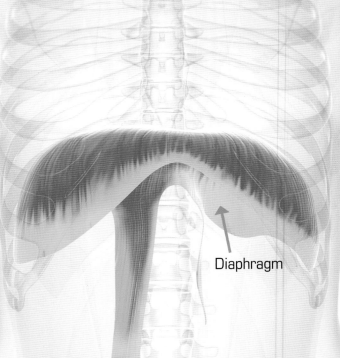

Diaphragm

Now, let's go back to the alveoli. Each alveolus has its own stem, called the alveolar duct. Alveoli are extremely small and have very thin walls. This allows for gases to diffuse across the membrane. The word diffusion is derived from the Latin word *diffundere*, which means "to spread out." Diffusion is movement of a substance from a region of high concentration to a region of low concentration. The gases that diffuse through the membrane are oxygen and carbon dioxide.

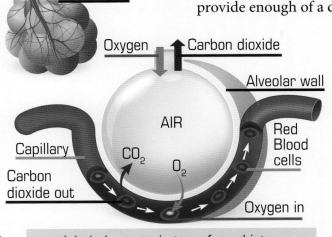

Oxygen · Carbon dioxide · Alveolar wall · AIR · Capillary · CO₂ · O₂ · Red Blood cells · Carbon dioxide out · Oxygen in

Inhaled oxygen is transferred into the blood while carbon dioxide is transferred to the alveoli to be exhaled.

Carbon dioxide (CO_2) is waste or garbage made as a result of all the chemical processes that occur in our bodies. The CO_2 travels through the bloodstream and arrives in the lungs. We exhale this CO_2. God has designed everything so that none of this is wasted! Trees and plants use the CO_2. In a happy trade, the plants release oxygen to us. We happily inhale the oxygen. The red blood cells act like mini cargo trucks by picking up the oxygen atoms to deliver them to the rest of the body.

Gas		Inhaled Air	Exhaled Air
Oxygen	O_2	21%	17%
Carbon Dioxide	CO_2	0.04%	4%
Nitrogen	N	78%	78%

Remarkably, the concentration of the air that enters the lungs compared to the air that exits the lungs seems relatively similar. Don't let the numbers fool you! These precise concentrations provide enough of a diffusional difference that the carbon dioxide and oxygen travel in opposite directions. There is still oxygen in the air we breathe out.

When we inhale, air travels all the way down through the bronchioles to the alveolar duct to the alveolar sacs. A large network of blood vessels and capillaries surround the alveolar sacs. The red blood cells course by in almost single file, dumping carbon dioxide and loading up on oxygen.

A special cell in the alveoli produces a substance called surfactant. Surfactant helps to keep the alveoli open by decreasing the tug that water vapor has on the walls of these balloon-like sacs.

Your respiratory system does a wonderful job of putting moisture in the air you breathe. As a result, water molecules line the walls of the alveolus. Water molecules are strongly attracted to each other. This attraction creates a force called surface tension. The alveoli decrease in size when you exhale and the surface tension increases. This force could cause the alveoli to collapse and stick tightly together. The force to peel the air sac walls apart would be difficult. Hard to imagine? Surface tension can be seen with the circus-like performance of an insect called the water strider. If you look at the surface of a pond you might see a water strider walking across the surface of the water without falling in due to the surface tension.

The Respiratory Lining

The outside of your body is covered with skin, so are the passageways of your respiratory tract. The "skin" lining is called the epithelium. Epithelium lines the surfaces of the body. The lining is found on every aspect of the respiratory tract from the mouth to the bronchioles.

There are several types of epithelium in the body. The epithelium that lines the respiratory tract is called ciliated pseudostratified columnar epithelium. This is simply a descriptive name for the tissue. It is ciliated — covered with hair-like structures. Pseudostratified refers to the cells appearing to be lined up somewhat in layers. The cells are shaped like columns. Easy peasy, right?

The respiratory lining in the lungs acts like the lint trap in your clothes dryer. It traps all the unwanted particles that enter your lungs. The hair cells — cilia — lie on top of the epithelium and the mucus lies on top of the cilia. The respiratory cilia beat in a coordinated manner upward, and particles that enter get trapped in the mucus. The mucus escalator acts like a conveyor belt to send things up and out.

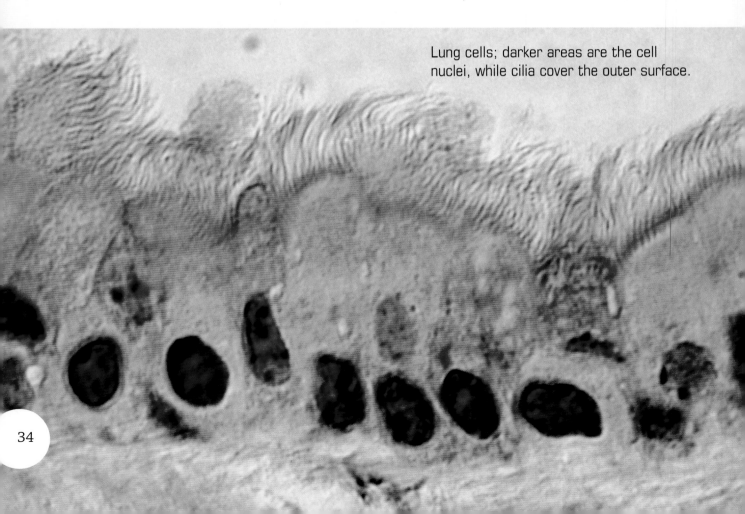

Lung cells; darker areas are the cell nuclei, while cilia cover the outer surface.

Carbon Monoxide Poisoning

Gases other than carbon dioxide and oxygen can diffuse through the alveolar wall. As the weather becomes colder, there is a higher incidence of carbon monoxide poisoning. The furnaces in homes kick on for the first time as the weather becomes colder. If furnaces are not well maintained they can produce a colorless, tasteless, and odorless gas called carbon monoxide. Carbon monoxide is found in the fumes produced in things like cars, trucks, fires, small gasoline engines, stoves, and heating systems.

The chemical formula for carbon dioxide is CO_2. It has one carbon molecule and two oxygen molecules attached together. Carbon monoxide is CO. It has one carbon and one oxygen molecule attached. Carbon monoxide is less dense and lighter than carbon dioxide. When it is inhaled, it diffuses more readily across the alveoli to the red blood cells in the lungs. Carbon monoxide pushes oxygen off the red blood cell and takes its spot. The tissues and organs of the body are unable to get oxygen. The carbon monoxide binds to the red blood cells. The person will begin to experience headache, tiredness, vomiting, confusion, and dizziness, and will eventually lose consciousness. To overcome this oxygen starvation the body experiences, the treatment is to give 100 percent oxygen to remove the carbon monoxide from the red blood cells.

This is why carbon monoxide detectors in the home are important. It is also important to maintain equipment and appliances, and have yearly furnace checks. Never use gasoline-powered equipment in areas that do not have good air circulation.

MEDI✚MOMENT

Deep sea diving provides a breathtaking opportunity to see incredible wonders that God has designed. Unlike the fish and other inhabitants of the deep, we were not designed to occupy such spaces. In order to go below the surface of the ocean, divers must breathe heavily pressurized gases to prevent their lungs from collapsing from the high pressures exerted on their bodies.

If divers ascend too quickly to the surface of the water after a deep dive, they can experience a potentially life-threatening condition called "the bends."

The bends or decompression sickness is caused by formation of bubbles of gas in the blood, like a carbonated soda. These bubbles of gas accumulate and travel in the bloodstream and form in the tissues. It is extremely painful. The gases can lodge in joints and in many places in the body, including the brain.

If the lungs were able to be filled with a liquid instead of a gas most of these problems could be avoided. In experimentation is the use of perfluorocarbon (PFC), a synthetic liquid that is clear and odorless. It has a high capacity to carry oxygen and carbon dioxide. It carries three times more oxygen and four times more carbon dioxide than air. The mixture actually sinks to the bottom of the lungs and opens up the alveoli. This liquid is being explored for utilization in life-threatening situations in the emergency room.

Respiration and ventilation are sometimes used interchangeably but the two words do not mean exactly the same thing. Respiration is the actual exchange of oxygen and carbon dioxide at the surface of the alveoli and capillaries in the lungs. Ventilation actually means the movement and flow of air in and out of the lungs. There are many terms used to measure the lung volumes and the movement of air in the lungs at different phases in the breathing process. These volumes can be measured utilizing a special device called a spirometer. Pulmonary Function Tests (PFTs) are a group of measurements that can assess how well the lungs take in and release air. (*Pulmo-* comes from Latin, and it means lung.) It evaluates how much oxygen breathed into the lungs actually enters the blood circulation for the body to use.

Pulmonary Function Testing is conducted in an enclosed booth, much like an old-fashioned telephone booth. A person seals their mouth around a mouthpiece and a plastic nose clip is applied. This ensures no air will escape from the nose and only the air from the mouth is measured. The mouthpiece is connected to the spirometer. It measures the flow of air when you exhale and the rate of the flow of air. These tests can be used to diagnose diseases of the lungs and monitor any changes in existing lung diseases.

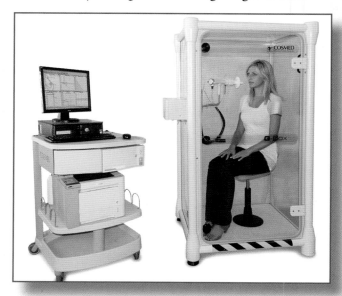

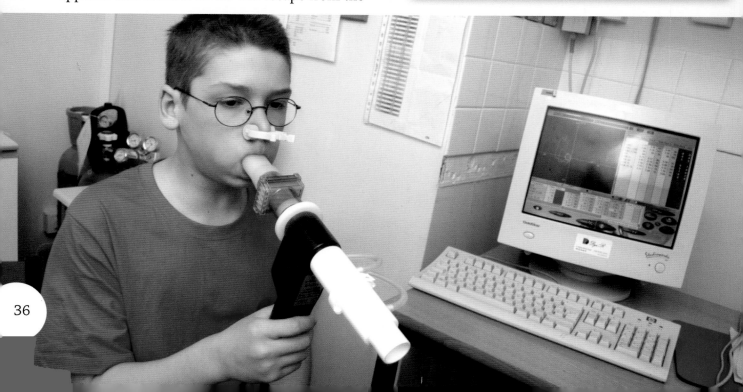

Averages In Men	
IRV	3.0
TV	.5
ERV	1.1
RV	1.2
TV + IRV + ERV = VC	
VC	4.6

Averages in Women	
IRV	3.0
TV	.5
ERV	1.1
RV	1.2
TV + IRV + ERV = VC	
VC	3.1

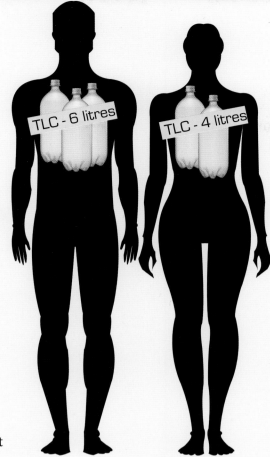

TLC - 6 litres

TLC - 4 litres

Take a deep breath! Being tested on a spirometer as we see here is an important tool for doctors to find out how well your lungs are working. Doctors might order a test like this to find out if your lungs are working properly, if you have a disease like bronchitis, or why you might be short of breath. Whether you are tested in a closed booth or with a specific type of spirometer (there are several different kinds), both will give the doctor a very clear reading (as shown above) to help diagnose where the problem may be. See the following page for other devices that help doctors figure out how well your respiratory system is working!

Volume	Definition
Total Lung Capacity (TLC)	The maximum amount of air that a person is capable of holding in their lungs, 4 to 6 liters of air in an adult
Inspiratory Reserve Volume (IRV)	The amount of air that can be taken in forcibly over the tidal volume, approximately 2 to 3 liters
Tidal Volume (TV)	The amount of air we breathe in and out when resting, about 500 mL
Expiratory Reserve Volume (ERV)	The amount of air that can be forced out of your lungs after you exhale a normal breath at rest
Residual Volume (RV)	The amount of air that remains in your lungs after you exhale
Vital Capacity (VC)	The total amount of air in your lungs TV+IRV+ERV

Other factors can impact your lung volume:

Larger volumes	Smaller volumes
People who are taller	People who are shorter
Healthy weight	Overweight
Healthy lungs	Chronic lung-related diseases or conditions
Born and living in high altitudes like the mountains	Born and living in lower altitudes like along the ocean

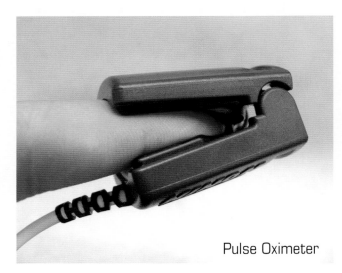

Pulse Oximeter

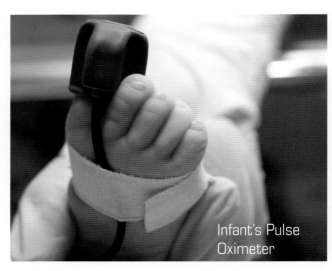

Infant's Pulse Oximeter

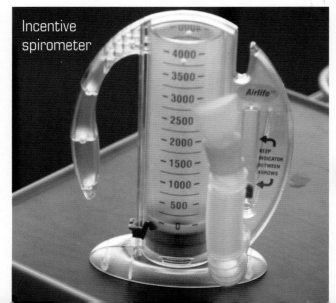

Incentive spirometer

- 4000 -
- 3500 -
- 3000 -
- 2500 -
- 2000 -
- 1500 -
- 1000 -
- 500 -
- 0

Airlife

KEEP INDICATOR BETWEEN ARROWS

A quick and easy way to see how much oxygen is in your blood is to use a pulse oximeter. It is usually slipped on the end of a person's finger. The pulse oximeter works by determining the percentage of oxygen absorption in the blood. It uses a red light. The amount of light absorbed depends on how much oxygen is bound in the red blood cells. An oxygen saturation (absorption) of 95% or higher is normal.

If the level is below 90 percent, it is considered dangerously low, or if it falls below 80, then your body's organs may not be functioning like they are supposed to, and you may need to be given oxygen in order to get better. As with any other aspect of your body, too little or too much is not good when it comes to oxygen in your bloodstream. God designed us to be perfectly balanced in making our wondrous machine work the very best!

People who have lung disease or have just undergone some kind of surgery are often given an incentive spirometer. This is used to help your lungs function better. Even some musicians who use wind instruments use them to improve the flow of air from their lungs. When using this device, you breathe in from the machine as slowly and deeply as you can. Then you hold your breath for several seconds — as many as 5 or 6 seconds. This helps open the alveoli. An indicator on the incentive spirometer notes how your lungs are working, and when used a number of times a day, you can improve your lungs functions.

Word Wise!

"GESUNDHEIT" is another customary response when one hears a sneeze. It is a German word and means "good" health!

Regulation of Breathing

Your rate of breathing changes depending on the needs of your body. Even your emotions can cause your respiratory rate to change. When you are fearful, you may hold your breath. During times of emotional distress, your rate of breathing may increase. When was the last time you had to remind yourself to breathe? You certainly can consciously decide to control when you breathe for periods of time.

Fortunately, God has designed our breathing under our voluntary and involuntary (occurs without you thinking) control. It would be incredibly distracting if you had to remember to breathe. There are two respiratory centers located specifically in the medulla oblongata of the brain. They are called the apneustic center and pneumotaxic center. The apneustic center controls the intensity of your breathing and its rate. The pneumotaxic center restricts the breathing in order to ensure that you don't overdistend your lungs with air. It also helps you maintain alternating between inspiration and expiration.

Chemoreceptors are additional respiratory regulators. They are located strategically in structures within the chest cavity. These sensors pick up on the chemistry of the blood. They take a chemical signal and send electrical impulses to the brain to adapt the respiratory rate as needed. Chemically, they detect the levels of carbon dioxide in the blood. If carbon dioxide increases in the blood the receptors will signal to the brain to increase the respiratory rate to get rid of more of this waste product from the body.

Pons
Medulla

Pneumotaxic Center
Apneustic Center
Expiratory Center
Inspiratory Center

Relation of diaphragm and intercostal muscles

Contraction of diaphragm and intercostal muscles

During the course of development in its mother's womb, a baby's lungs are not necessary for life. The lungs' ability to function upon leaving the womb is vital to life as the child greets the world. The organogenesis of the lungs begins at four weeks' gestation. Gestation is the period of development in the mother's womb from conception to birth. *Organ* refers to an organ and *genesis* refers to the origin or beginning of something. As the Bible states in Genesis in the Bible, God created the earth and its inhabitants in only six days. The organogenesis of the lungs takes place over the entire 40 weeks of gestation.

The production of amniotic fluid in the womb that surrounds the baby is important to the development of the lungs. Amniotic fluid is "inhaled" and "exhaled" by the baby. The baby does not actually breathe in this watery environment. This fluid, which goes in and out of the lungs, assists in lung development, protects the baby, and allows for freer movement in the womb. In addition to the amniotic fluid, surfactant is produced by the type 2 cells of the lungs. The type 2 cells do not begin manufacturing surfactant until 26 weeks' gestation.

This image has been put together from the scans of a 12-week-old fetus. In addition to the parts of the skeletal system seen (skull, spine, rib cage) in white, you can also identify the two lungs, shown in purple, above the kidneys highlighted in bright pink.

I AM wonderfully made!

Unlike other organs that develop in the womb, the lungs are organs that are not needed for breathing, yet they have to be ready to work at the moment of birth. Lungs develop throughout the entire period in the mother's womb and for some months after being born. What amazing planning has been built into God's design of our bodies to function when and how they should!

The phases of lung development are depicted below.

Phrase	Development in the Womb	Illustration
Embryonic phase	4–5 weeks; first segments of the lungs appear at this time	
Pseudoglandular phase	Occurs between 5 and 16 weeks; the entire conducting tunnels of air are completed from the trachea all the way to the terminal bronchiole	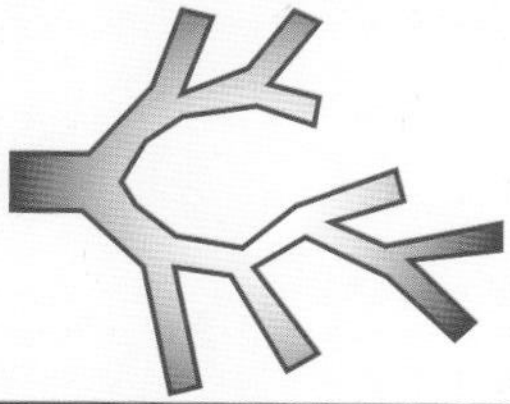
Canalicular Phase	Occurs between 16 and 26 weeks. The actual respiration parts develop: the lung tissue, alveolar sacs, and type 1 and 2 cells.	
Saccular Phase	This phase occurs from 26 weeks to birth. The grape-like clusters of the alveoli develop at the ends of the terminal bronchioles.	
Alveolar Phase	This occurs in the last couple of weeks of pregnancy. Only a third of the 300 million alveoli have grown to completion. The number of alveoli increases dramatically over the first 6 months after birth. This growth of alveoli continues for the first year and a half.	

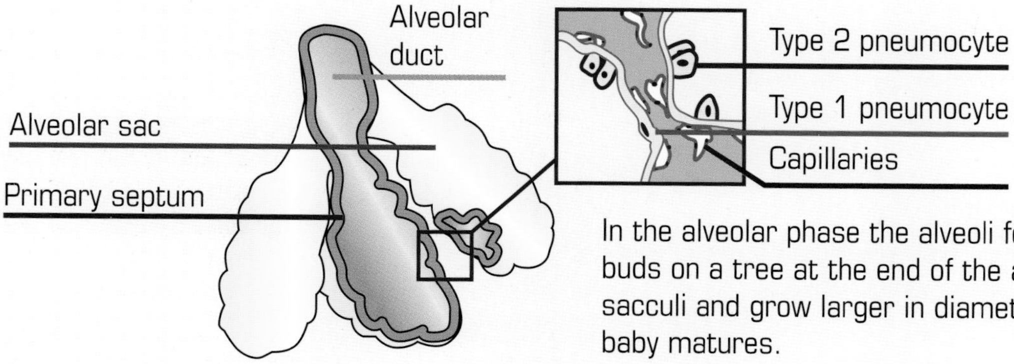

Alveolar duct

Alveolar sac

Primary septum

Type 2 pneumocyte

Type 1 pneumocyte

Capillaries

In the alveolar phase the alveoli form like little buds on a tree at the end of the alveolar sacculi and grow larger in diameter as the baby matures.

41

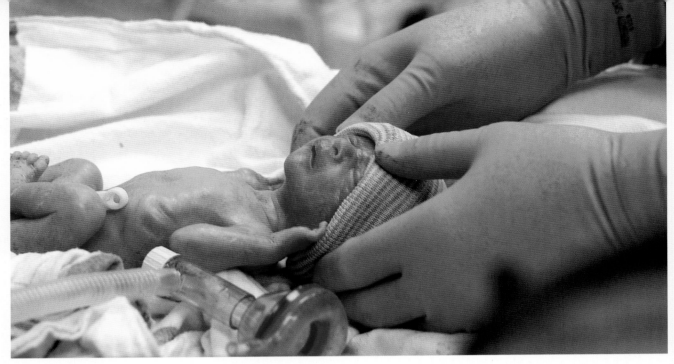

Sometimes babies are born early. The lungs of a baby may not be ready to fully function if born prior to 36 weeks of gestation. Their lungs may be immature and the baby's body has limited muscle strength and energy for effective breathing. Often they lack a substance that makes them unable to overcome the surface tension in their alveoli. If a mother goes into early labor during pregnancy, doctors may give the mother steroids, a medicine that can help the baby have better lung function on delivery.

Respiratory distress is a term used to describe someone who is having difficulty breathing. How a person attempts to overcome breathing difficulty can look and sound different, depending on the age of the person. For example, if you were to stand up and go for a run around the block as fast as you could, more than likely you would be out of breath. You would instinctively do maneuvers to help yourself grab a bigger breath of air. For example, you might bend over and put your hands on your knees. This allows you to lift up your ribs in an attempt to retrieve more air. Your nostrils would flare and your head might bob up and down with each breath. When someone is in respiratory distress, they may appear the same way.

A baby who is unable to sit up cannot do these types of maneuvers if he is having difficulty breathing. In order to force air into his lungs, a sick baby in respiratory distress may actually grunt. This is a worrisome sign. Take a quick moment and give it a try. Make the sound of a quick grunt. Try it again. What do your lungs feel like when you do a forceful grunt? The grunt increases the pressure in the alveoli in an attempt to fully open them to take in more oxygen. The grunt is a way that the baby increases his PEEP. Not a peep like a baby chick. PEEP stands for Positive End Expiratory Pressure. This is the positive pressure that is exerted in the alveoli at the end of exhalation.

Word Wise!

SACCULI is Latin for a small sac. This word was used in the 1600s to mean a small bag or sack of herbs applied to the body.

MEDI✚MOMENT

Enterovirus-D68 (EV-D68) sounds like the name of some science fiction space craft. This could not be further from the truth. It is actually a virus that can make you sick. There are many different types of enteroviruses — over 100 types.

Early in the fall of 2014, an outbreak of EV-D68 occurred in the United States, causing many children to become ill with respiratory symptoms. This virus was first identified in California in 1962. Of the very ill, many required care in the intensive care units of hospitals, a place for the sickest of patients. This enterovirus had some characteristics similar to the polio virus from long ago. Not only did children experience respiratory problems but in rare cases they were accompanied by weakness eerily similar to the polio outbreak of the 1950s.

Purdue University has used a special technique, X-ray crystallography, to discover the exact structure of EV-D68. They are currently studying the effects of binding it to an anti-viral compound in hopes of finding a treatment.

A vaccine has not yet been developed to prevent EV-D68, nor is there a specific medication to combat it. There are specialized tests to determine if the enterovirus is EV-D68, but it is not readily available in most places. And despite the success of current antibiotics on other illnesses, they do not work for EV-D68 or other viruses.

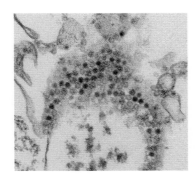

Leaning over and holding your hands on your knees can help you get more air after a hard run or busy exercise.

Do you sneeze at sunlight? One in four people experience photic sneezing when they go out into sunlight!

43

If you lived in the 18th century and had a cough, your mother might have reached for a "common" remedy. Steaming hot barley boiled in a pot mixed with water, snail slime, and a touch of brown sugar would fix you up in a jiffy. Not really? Well, you are probably right. Prior to the turn of the century, our technology and knowledge were limited when it came to effective ways to evaluate and treat the lungs. Today there are many ways that doctors can assess our lungs to see how they are working.

Breath sounds are either normal or abnormal. Fluid in the lungs, heart failure, asthma and even pneumonia will alter the normal sounds of the lungs

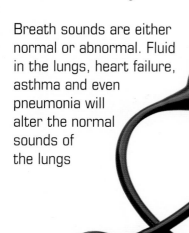

The Stethoscope

The stethoscope is a tried and faithful tool of the doctor. It is used to listen to the sounds of the body, from the beating heart to the air moving through the lungs to the rumbling of the stomach. It is the oldest of tools and was invented by physician Theophile René Laennec, who demonstrated the use of a tube for investigating the lungs and heart. He realized that one could listen to sounds through a tube. It was improper for a doctor to place his head on a woman's chest to listen to heart sounds, he rolled a piece of paper into a tube and placed it over the area of her heart to listen. He invented it in 1819. In 1855, George Phillip Cammann, an American doctor, took Laennec's idea and developed the stethoscope we know today.

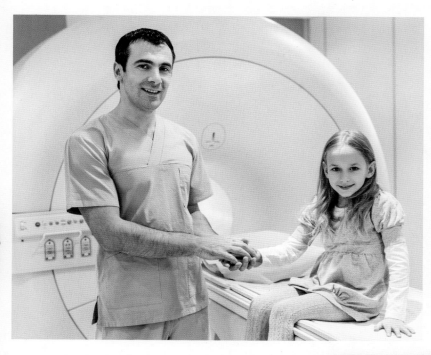

PET or Positron Emission Tomography Scan is a type of imaging study. In order to perform the scan, a small amount of radioactive dye called a tracer is injected into a vein in the arm. The dye travels in the body and collects in areas of the lungs. The patient is placed on a table and slid into a large scanner. A computer takes the images of the lungs and generates 3-D pictures. This test can evaluate how well the lungs and the tissues are working.

Computed Tomography Scan (CT Scan)

The CT scan stands for computed tomography. CT scans are excellent tools to look at images of the lungs. Multiple images are taken in cross-sectional segments of the lungs. The slices are much like slicing a hard boiled egg. Placing a hard-boiled egg in an egg slicer and pressing down on the lever. The egg is perfectly evenly sliced. You are able to look at the inside of the yolk in various locations. This is similar to the images taken in a CT scan, but no actual physical cuts are made in the body. The computer generates these images. This scan is helpful in the diagnosis of diseases of the lungs, for example, to possibly assist in finding the causes of a persistent cough, shortness of breath, or chest pain.

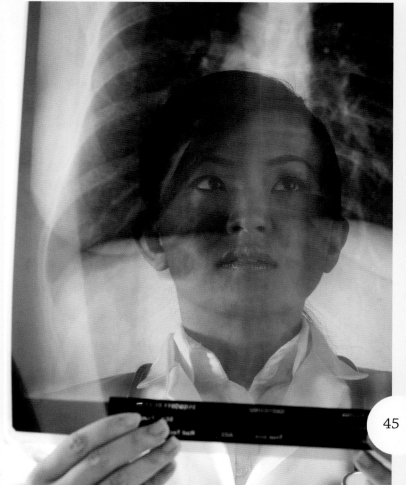

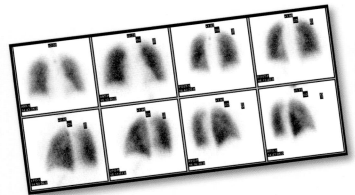

Normal pulmonary ventilation and perfusion (V/Q) scan. The nuclear medicine V/Q scan is useful in the evaluation of pulmonary embolism.

Pulmonary Perfusion Scan

Air flows in and out of the lungs. The function of the lungs can become limited if something blocks the flow of oxygen into the bloodstream. The Pulmonary Perfusion Scan measures air and blood flow in your lungs. It compares the ventilation (where air flows in the lungs) and the perfusion (where the blood flows in the lungs). This type of scan is very helpful in identifying a possible pulmonary embolism. Let's break that down a bit.

Pulmonary means anything pertaining to the lungs. Embolism originates from the Greek word *embolus* which means "plug" or "stopper." An embolism is a clot of blood that hardens in the blood stream and breaks off. It usually travels up from the vein of a leg and plugs up an artery in the lung. This blocks blood from flowing to that part of the lung.

This test compares the perfusion to the ventilation. In a pulmonary embolism, the ventilation is high (air is moving in the lung passageways) as the person tries to breathe, but the perfusion (the blood flow to that area) is low due to the clot blocking the flow.

Pulmonary Embolism

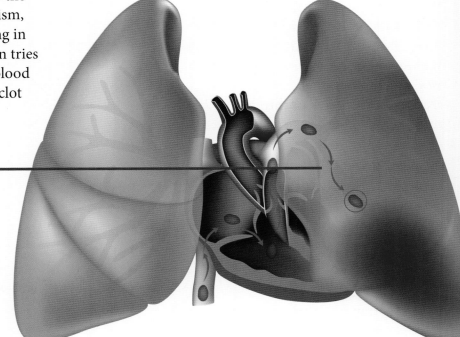

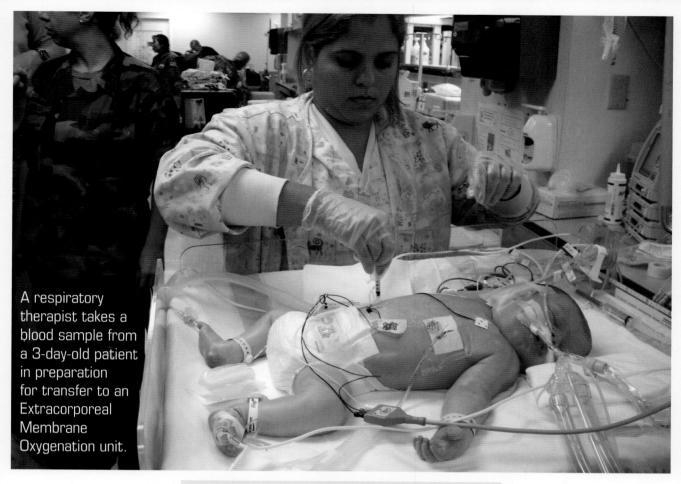

A respiratory therapist takes a blood sample from a 3-day-old patient in preparation for transfer to an Extracorporeal Membrane Oxygenation unit.

ECMO (Extracorporeal Membrane Oxygenation)

ECMO, or Extracorporeal Membrane Oxygenation, is a procedure that can be used in some of the smallest and sickest of patients whose heart and lungs cannot function normally on their own. The ECMO machine performs most of the work and allows for the heart and lungs to work more easily. Special tubes allow the blood from the patient to pass through the ECMO machine where the blood is oxygenated and carbon dioxide is removed like an artificial lung. The blood is returned to the patient. This type of invasive procedure can only be utilized for a few weeks. It allows time for the body to heal.

Unfortunately, there are people whose lungs are so damaged that their lungs will not recover. ECMO is a short-term solution to serious lung and heart problems. Individuals who are waiting for a lung transplant from a donor cannot use this technology. Dr. Robert Barlett, a surgeon at the University of Michigan Medical Center, is part of a research team trying to develop an artificial lung. It is called the BioLung.

The BioLung does not use a mechanical pump. The blood from the patient doesn't even leave their body. The heart of the patient continues to beat. The BioLung is packed with special hollow plastic fibers with teeny tiny holes that allow only gas to pass through. Similar to real lungs, these fibers allow carbon dioxide to leave the blood, and oxygen is allowed to enter. This oxygenated blood is in the heart and can then be pumped to all the organs of the body. The BioLung is still in development. It holds great promise for those whose lungs no longer work well.

Take Good Care

Therefore, I urge you, brothers and sisters, in view of God's mercy, to offer your bodies as a living sacrifice, holy and pleasing to God — this is your true and proper worship (Romans 12:1).

We are told here by Paul to surrender our all to God. As believers in Christ, we are to be a "living" sacrifice. No longer, as we were commanded in the Old Testament, do we offer animal sacrifices to God. We offer ourselves. We are tempted by many things and pleasures in life. We have the ability to desire many things in excess, from food to things that may be damaging to our bodies. These things hold promises of short-term enjoyment with lifetime damage. In order to serve God effectively, we have to be good stewards of what He has given us, including our bodies.

God has given us a wonderful gift. We are to care for our bodies. Here are three helpful tips for keeping your lungs healthy:

It was once believed the breath was the soul. It was once thought that your soul escaped your body during a sneeze, and saying "God bless you" would keep the devil from taking your soul before it could get back safely.

on the nose.

Don't smoke

Get plenty of exercise

Eat a healthy diet

Smoking and Your Lungs

We continue to expand our knowledge of what God has created around us and in us. Smoking has proven to be very damaging to the lungs. Smoking has gone in and out of favor in public circles through the years. Today, smoking is prohibited in most public areas. Today, we understand the damage that smoking causes to the lungs.

In the late 1600s, King James II of England despised smoking. He hated it so much that anyone who was caught smoking was treated as a criminal. The offender would be thrown in jail if caught committing this horrible crime.

Smoking is a very difficult habit to break once you get started. Many people who practiced this habit were addicted. (An addiction occurs when one becomes enslaved to a habit or practice despite the negative consequences.) People began to find new ways to satisfy their addiction in order not to be found guilty of a crime. They began chewing tobacco. One of the unsavory products of chewing tobacco is that much tobacco "juice" is produced. If one swallows this "juice," they experience a great deal of intestinal unrest and spew their stomach contents.

Enter stage left — the spittoon or cuspidor. A spittoon or cuspidor is a container used for spitting into. In years past, you could find a spittoon just about any place: stores, saloons, banks, hotels, and even at churches. Spittoons were considered the polite way to practice spitting in public. It was far more hygienic to spit in a spittoon than on the floor. It is known that President Andrew Jackson (1767–1845) wanted to care for guests, and he had 20 spittoons placed in various places throughout the White House.

Skillfully spitting into a spittoon was a great gift, although certainly not one of the spiritual gifts. A true virtuoso was able to create the melodious sound of a "pinger." A "pinger" is the loud crescendo sound made when a tight wad of wet tobacco hits the inside of a metal spittoon.

Today, we know that smoking causes 90 percent of the cases of lung cancer. We also know that the nicotine in cigarettes is incredibly addicting. In times past, it was commonplace to see advertisements for cigarettes on TV. In April 1970, Congress passed the Public Health Cigarette Smoking Act, banning the advertisement of cigarettes on TV.

49

What do cigarettes do to the lungs?

1. The lungs lose their ability to be elastic and stretchy. Normally, as you breathe, your lungs expand and decrease in size to accommodate the volume of air. Smoking damages the tissue by depositing a sticky substance called tar. It becomes very difficult to exhale (breathe out).

2. Smoking causes a great deal of mucus to be manufactured. This mucus clogs the airways. It is common for smokers to experience the "smoker's cough." This is their body's attempt to dislodge the sticky mucus to clear the air passages.

3. The cilia, (hair cells), of the lungs cannot clear dirt and chemicals that become caught in the airways. The air sacs in the lungs are unable to function, and many will actually break open due to excessive pressure.

4. It causes cancer in the lungs as well as other lung diseases like emphysema, asthma, and chronic obstructive pulmonary disease (COPD). All of these diseases prevent the lungs from working properly. Smoking also causes heart disease and bladder cancer.

The costs of smoking are many. An individual does not only pay with their health, but also out of their pocketbook. The average pack of cigarettes costs $6. Depending on how much a person smokes a day, this could amount to $89 a month — a staggering $1,068 a year.

In April of 1994, according to the United States Department of Health and Human Services, five major American cigarette companies submitted a list of ingredients in cigarettes. The master list reveals that 599 ingredients are added to cigarettes. Many of these additives are carcinogens. (A carcinogen is a substance that is known to cause cancer in humans or animals.) Take a look at the list below of some of the known additives that are found in cigarettes. See if you recognize any that you would want to put into your body.

Additive	Where it is typical found
Arsenic	poison, used in rat poisons
Formaldehyde	used to preserve dead specimens and for embalming
Naphthalene	moth balls
Ammonia	household cleaner
Cadmium	used in batteries
DDT	a banned insecticide
Polonium-20	a cancer-causing, nuclear waste radioactive element
Acetylene	fuel used in torches
Benzene	gasoline additive
Carbon Monoxide	car exhaust
Hexamine	explosive ingredient
Methanol	rocket fuel

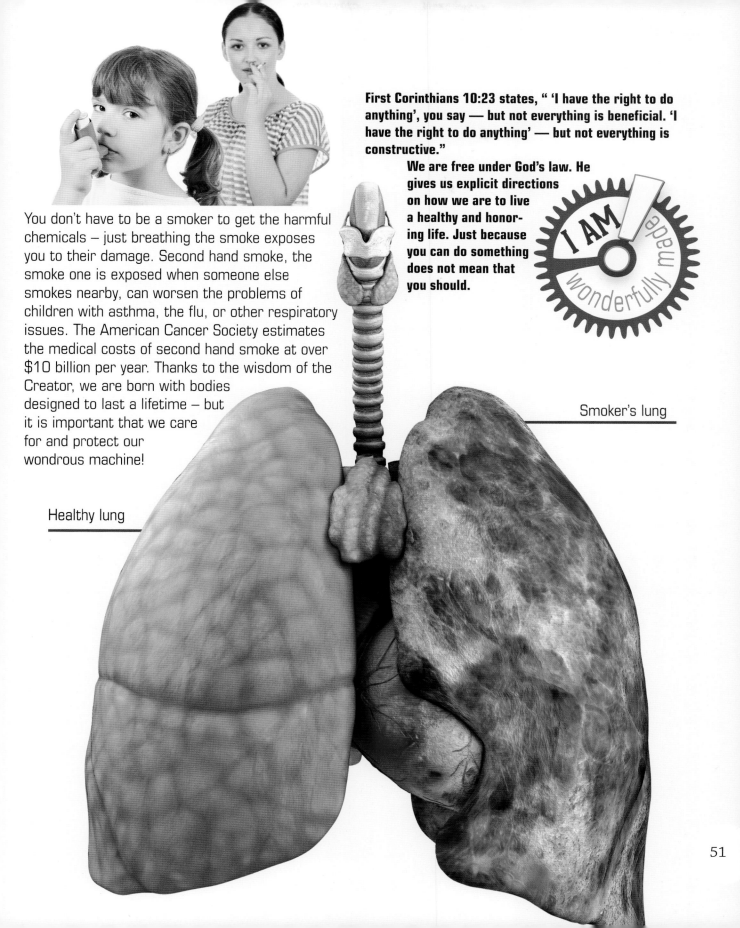

You don't have to be a smoker to get the harmful chemicals — just breathing the smoke exposes you to their damage. Second hand smoke, the smoke one is exposed when someone else smokes nearby, can worsen the problems of children with asthma, the flu, or other respiratory issues. The American Cancer Society estimates the medical costs of second hand smoke at over $10 billion per year. Thanks to the wisdom of the Creator, we are born with bodies designed to last a lifetime — but it is important that we care for and protect our wondrous machine!

First Corinthians 10:23 states, " 'I have the right to do anything', you say — but not everything is beneficial. 'I have the right to do anything' — but not everything is constructive."

We are free under God's law. He gives us explicit directions on how we are to live a healthy and honoring life. Just because you can do something does not mean that you should.

I AM wonderfully made

Smoker's lung

Healthy lung

51

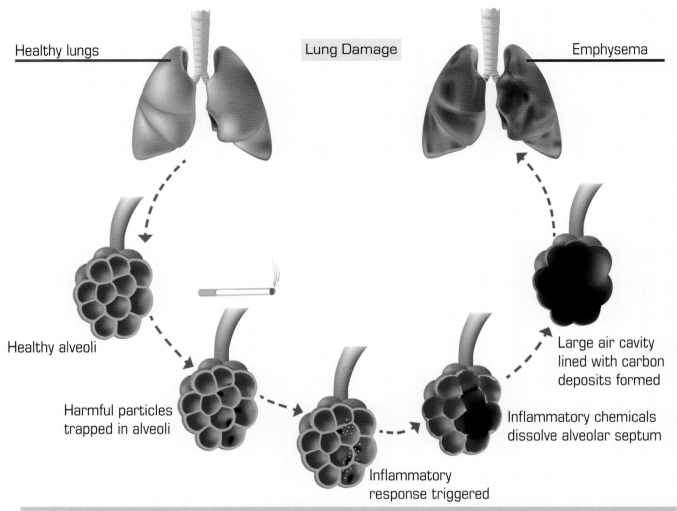

Healthy lungs

Lung Damage

Emphysema

Healthy alveoli

Harmful particles
trapped in alveoli

Inflammatory
response triggered

Inflammatory chemicals
dissolve alveolar septum

Large air cavity
lined with carbon
deposits formed

Quitting Smoking: Now that we have seen some of the bad news about smoking, it's time for some good news. Once the hard and challenging decision to quit smoking occurs, the ex-smoker will begin to experience the positive effects of stopping.

20 minutes after one's last cigarette	The blood pressure and pulse decrease.
	The temperature in the hands and feet increases.
8 hours after one's last cigarette	The blood in the body begins to recover and the levels of carbon monoxide decreases. The oxygen levels return to normal.
48 hours after one's last cigarette	The nerve endings in the mouth and nose begin to regenerate sense of taste, and smell improves.
A few weeks after one's last cigarette	The lung function improves.
1 year after one's last cigarette	The risk of heart disease has been cut in half.
5 years after one's last cigarette	The risk of stroke, bleeding in the brain, is decreased.
15 years after one's last cigarette	The person's risk of heart disease is now comparable to someone who never smoked a single cigarette in his or her life.

Illnesses of the Lungs

Germs That Make You Squirm

There are things that we put in our bodies that can cause damage to them. However, there are other infectious agents, germy critters like bacteria and viruses, that can cause illness to the body. God has equipped our bodies with defenses to fight against uninvited guests. He has made special cells, proteins, tissues, and organs in our bodies to fight against germs. The major cells that help fight against disease are white blood cells. They are the military intelligence and soldiers that go to battle. As our soldiers are battling within our bodies, we can experience symptoms while the war rages. Viruses and bacteria can produce similar symptoms like vomiting, diarrhea, fever, rashes, and cough. These symptoms are ways that our bodies attempt to show these infectious agents the door.

Viruses and bacteria have some basic differences. Viruses are 100 times smaller than a single bacteria. A bacteria is 10 times smaller than a single human cell. Viruses are not alive by themselves and cannot survive long outside the body. Viruses and bacteria enter the body via the mouth, nose, or open wounds. A virus enters the body and hijacks the cells. It causes the cell to use its machinery to produce more viruses. The viruses are mass produced and fill the cell until it ruptures open. The newly formed viruses try to take over other cells. Bacteria, on the other hand, can survive outside the body for a longer period of time and are more complex than viruses. Most of the earth's biomass is made up of bacteria — it is believed to be about 5 nonillion (5×10 to the 30th power by USA measurement!). Some bacteria are very helpful and even aid in our digestion. Only about 1 percent of all bacteria cause disease.

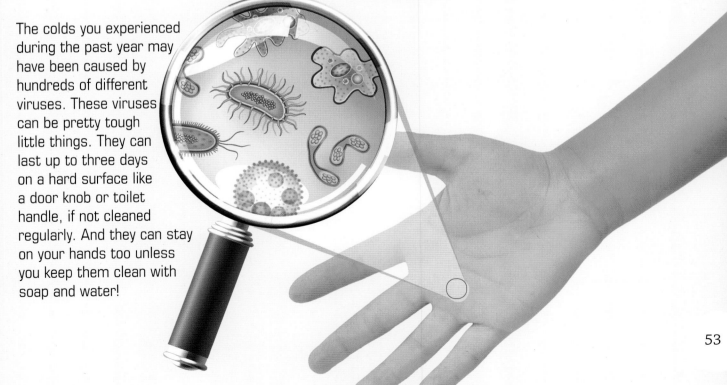

The colds you experienced during the past year may have been caused by hundreds of different viruses. These viruses can be pretty tough little things. They can last up to three days on a hard surface like a door knob or toilet handle, if not cleaned regularly. And they can stay on your hands too unless you keep them clean with soap and water!

53

Epidemic vs Pandemic

We have seen great outbreaks of disease and illness over the ages that affect the lungs. The word, epidemic, is used to refer to increased outbreaks of disease that affect a particular region or area. A pandemic occurs when there is an outbreak of a disease that expands over large geographic areas and continents.

Every winter there is always an increase in respiratory illnesses. One of the biggest factors that contributes to this increased occurrence of illness is that many people stay indoors and are in close confines with one another. Good hand washing, covering your mouth or nose when you cough or sneeze, and staying home from school/work when you are sick is important in decreasing other's exposures to illness.

The Flu Can Make You Blue

Major outbreaks of Influenza have occurred over the years. Influenza is the same thing we call the "flu." It is caused by a virus. People who suffer from influenza experience fever, cough, sore throat, runny nose, body aches, headaches, and tiredness. At the end of World War I in 1918, influenza was a wartime killer that claimed the lives of 40 million people. Nearly half the world's population was infected. This was indeed a pandemic.

Word Wise!

"STERNUTATION" means to sneeze.

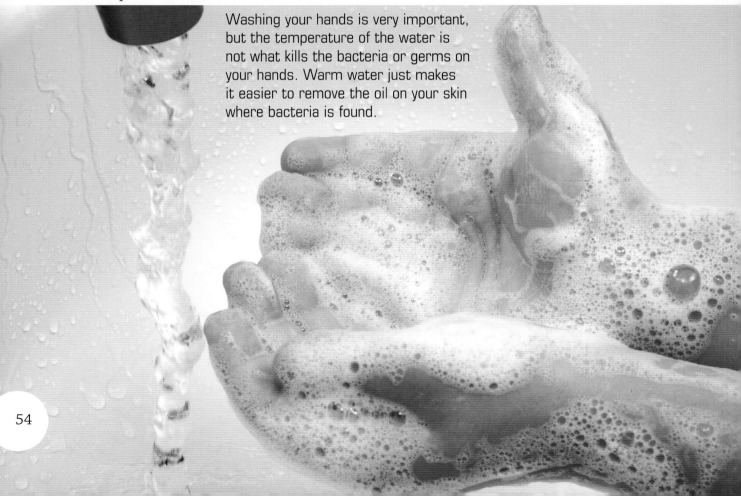

Washing your hands is very important, but the temperature of the water is not what kills the bacteria or germs on your hands. Warm water just makes it easier to remove the oil on your skin where bacteria is found.

54

Tuberculosis

Tuberculosis (TB) is a disease caused by a bacterium called *Mycobacterium tuberculosis*. It is a highly contagious disease. ("Contagious" refers to something that is easily spread from one person to another.) TB is spread by droplets from coughing, sneezing, talking, or spit. It typically affects the lungs, but can also infect other parts of the body like the spine, brain, or kidney. It was the leading cause of death in the United States in the early 1900s. Due to the highly infectious nature of TB, sanitariums were erected in the United States. Sanitariums are places where individuals who suffer from contagious diseases are isolated from society in long-term medical facilities. These facilities were referred to as "waiting rooms for death."

In 1904, The National Association for the Study and Prevention of Tuberculosis was founded to lead the fight against tuberculosis. They began the Christmas Seal campaign in 1907 to raise money for a small TB sanitarium in Delaware. This organization's name was later changed to the one many know it by today, the American Lung Association. The tagline for its campaigns to promote good lung health was "It's a matter of life and breath." Today, its tagline is "Fighting for Air."

This is a far cry from the image that TB had in the 1700 and 1800s. Back then TB was called "consumption" because as the disease ravaged the body, the individual lost a great deal of weight and the disease consumed them. During those times, to have TB was considered to be very fashionable. It tended to kill many famous, wealthy, and incredibly talented people. There were romantic painters who depicted TB as an elegant disease. The person would appear pale and gaunt with rosy cheeks.

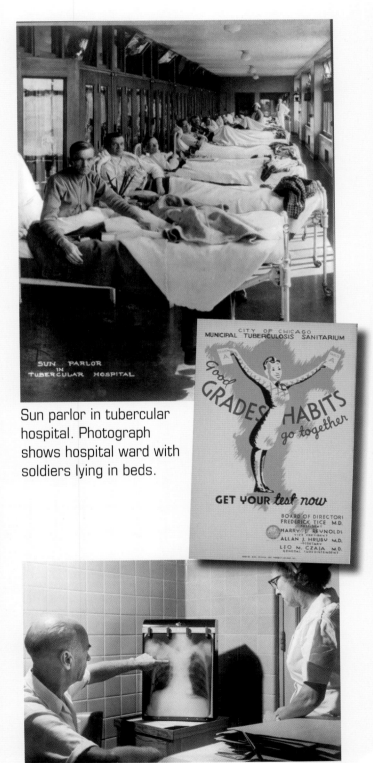

Sun parlor in tubercular hospital. Photograph shows hospital ward with soldiers lying in beds.

If a skin or blood test reveals TB bacteria, a chest x-ray or sputum sample may show TB disease.

Cystic Fibrosis

Cystic fibrosis is an inherited disease. It is a disease passed from parent to child in their genetic instructions. The complexity and precision with which God designed the body blows our minds. A small addition, change, or deletion in the genetic instructions in the body can cause huge malfunctions. Cystic fibrosis is a result of a specific genetic defect that interferes with the body's ability to carry salt and water to and from the cells. Due to this defect, many organ systems in the body are impaired. Thick, gummy mucus builds up and clogs the lungs and the digestive tracts. It affects the lungs, pancreas, liver, intestines, sinuses, and reproductive organs, the areas that are high producers of mucus in the body.

The host of problems that cystic fibrosis patients suffer from was observed by Dr. Dorothy Andersen, a pathologist at Columbia-Presbyterian Babies and Children's Hospital in New York in 1938. (A pathologist is a medical doctor specialist who studies tissue samples, blood, and fluid from patients in order to make diagnoses about illnesses.) In her studies of these patients, she noted that several systems of the body were involved. These patients experienced thick, sticky mucus clogging their lung passageways. They became sick more often and were extremely susceptible to infections of the lungs. The mucus blocked the ducts in their pancreas, which prevented the pancreatic enzymes from exiting the pancreas. These enzymes are important in helping in the digestion of food, in particular fats, proteins, and carbohydrates. The patients' appetites were great, but they suffered from malnutrition. The sweat glands in their skin did not work well, and they had a salty taste to their skin. This was noted when parents kissed their child.

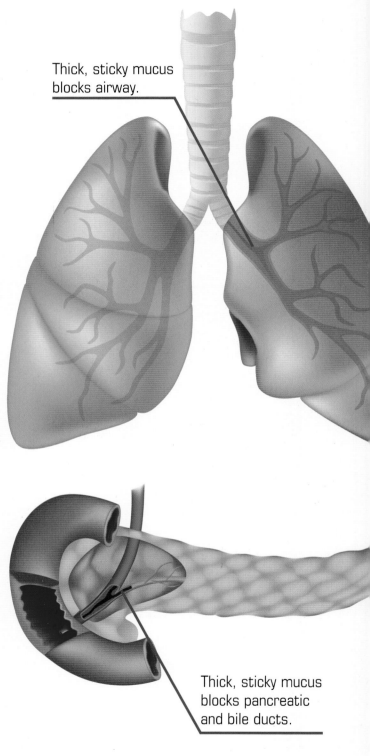

Thick, sticky mucus blocks airway.

Thick, sticky mucus blocks pancreatic and bile ducts.

The specific gene, cystic fibrosis transmembrane conductance regulator, or CFTR, that causes cystic fibrosis was discovered in 1989. The disease occurs primarily in those of northern European descent — 1 out of 3,500 white children. The disease is much less common in non-white children with 1 out of 12,000 affected. Some diseases may continue to occur because they have some protective qualities against other ailments. Diarrhea was a common cause of death in early times, but still remains a threat in Third World countries. Those who carry the defect in the CFTR gene are less affected by deadly diarrheal illnesses but tormented by the effects of the genetic disorder.

CFTR Gene
Chromosome 7

Dr. Paul di Sant'Agnese developed an effective technique of diagnosing cystic fibrosis in 1953. He developed the "gold standard" for diagnosis called the "sweat test." The sweat test measures the concentration of chloride in the sweat. It is a painless test. There are two parts to it. First, a chemical that has no odor or color is placed on a small area of the skin, usually the arm or leg. An electrode with a very weak electrical charge is placed on top of the area. The combination of the chemical and the electrode causes the area to sweat. This step lasts for about five minutes. Second, the area is cleaned and the sweat is collected. The sweat is sent to a specialty lab to measure the amount of chloride found in the sample.

IPPB (Intermittent Positive Pressure Breathing) therapy for Cystic Fibrosis is a therapy utilized in patients who have difficulty with their lungs. It delivers a controlled pressure of a gas to help in air movement and expansion of the lungs. Aerosol medications can be given with the treatment.

Allergic Rhinitis or Hay Fever

Achoo! Sniff! The warm sun beats down. The flowers are in full bloom. *Sniff!* It is a glorious time of the year. *Achoo!* Yep, allergy season is in full bloom also. (An allergy is an exaggerated reaction of the immune system to a foreign body.)

Allergic rhinitis, or, as it is "affectionately" called, hay fever, tends to hit people who suffer from it in the spring. It is an allergic response to the stuff that floats through the air causing inflammation of the nasal airways. The stuff that causes such a reaction is called allergens. An allergen can be anything such as dust mites (little critters that can live between the sheets of bedding), tree and grass pollens, fungi, molds, dust, or animal dander (the particles of hair and skin shed by an animal). The immune system kicks into high gear and becomes overreactive to these irritants.

Symptoms can consist of increased mucus production in the nasal passages accompanied by rhinorrhea (runny nose), sneezing, watery eyes, and pressure in the sinus cavities. A unique characteristic of children suffering from this type of seasonal allergy is the "allergic salute." Children aren't always known for grabbing a tissue when their noses are runny. Frankly, anything will do to wipe the nose . . . a shirt or even the hand. Habitually, the palm of the hand is rubbed upward at the opening of the nose, and the motion looks like a salute. Due to this constant "saluting," it is not uncommon to see a crease near the bridge of the nose. When doctors spot this crease they see it as a helpful clue in potentially identifying an allergy sufferer.

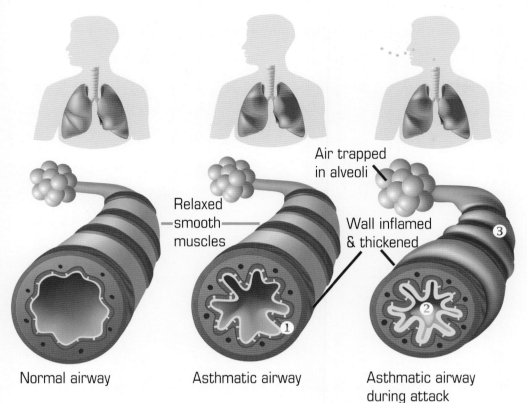

Relaxed smooth muscles

Air trapped in alveoli

Wall inflamed & thickened

① ② ③

Normal airway

Asthmatic airway

Asthmatic airway during attack

In an asthma attack, three things occur to the lung passageways.

1. The lining of the airways becomes inflamed and swollen. This swelling narrows the passageway.

2. The lungs increase production of mucus. This mucus clogs the airways, further narrowing the area.

3. The tiny straps of smooth muscle that encircle the bronchioles spasm and tighten around the tubes.

Asthma

Asthma is a chronic lung disease that is in the same family of illnesses as allergic rhinitis. In fact, many people who suffer from asthma also suffer from allergic rhinitis. What is asthma anyway? Asthma is a reversible, recurring inflammation of the lung passageways. It tends to run in families. An asthma "attack" can occur in response to environmental things, allergies, exercise, or infections. During an asthma "attack," a person becomes acutely short of breath and experiences chest tightness and wheezing. Wheezing is a high-pitched sound made as the person breathes. Coughing occurs due to the mucus that accumulates in the narrowed airways. Do you have asthma or know someone who does? According to the National Heart, Lung, and Blood Institute, approximately 25 million people in the United States suffer from asthma; 7 million of those are children.

Asthma Gadgets

Many asthmatics will describe their symptoms as feeling like an elephant is sitting on their chest or that a vise is squeezing their chest, trapping the air inside. If you were to take a straw, pinch it a bit, and try to breathe exclusively out of it, you would experience difficulty breathing similar to what a person with asthma experiences. Asthma can be serious and even life-threatening if it is not properly treated. There is no cure for asthma. Fortunately, there are many things that can be used to treat the symptoms. There are a multitude of inhalation medications. The medication can be delivered through an inhaler or a nebulizer. The inhaler is portable and can be carried anywhere. The nebulizer is placed in a mouthpiece container and the medication is suspended in the air in tiny droplets via an electrical compressor. The nebulizer is great for small children or people who are having great difficulty taking a good breath.

Native Americans boiled cherry bark and drank it as a tea to treat coughs. This bark contains hydrocyanic acid, an ingredient found in modern cold remedies that helps stop coughing. It's just one example of God providing us with natural resources we can use for medicines and improvements in our lives!

on the nose.

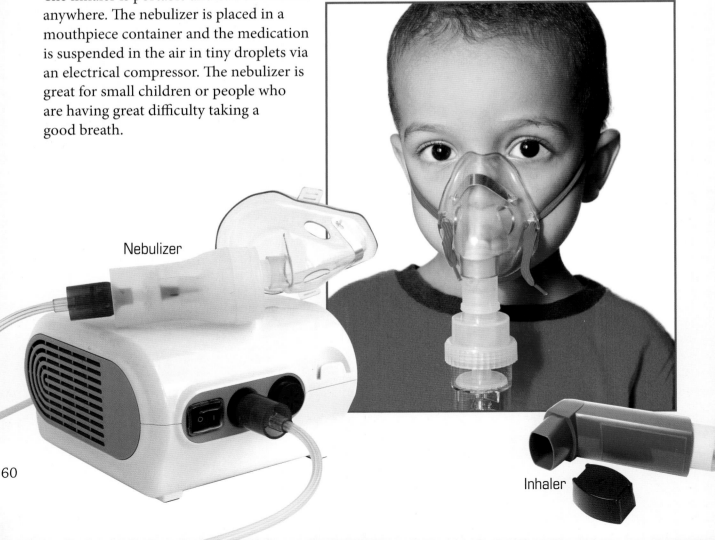

Nebulizer

Inhaler

60

Laryngitis

Laryngitis is inflammation of the larynx. Swelling occurs in the area of the vocal cords. It is caused by viral and bacterial infections. In addition, singers, coaches, and enthusiastic sports fans can experience overuse of their vocal cords, causing pain and inflammation. The throat feels "scratchy" and the voice is hoarse. One illness you may have heard of is laryngotracheobronchitis. Whew, let's break that down in common layman's terms. Laryngotracheobronchitis is also known as "the croup." Typically, this illness occurs in the winter months in young children. The child's cough sounds like a seal barking. Most cases of croup are caused by viruses. Treatment is aimed at comforting the sufferer and allowing the body to heal itself. Air humidifiers, hot showers, and drinking plenty of fluids are helpful.

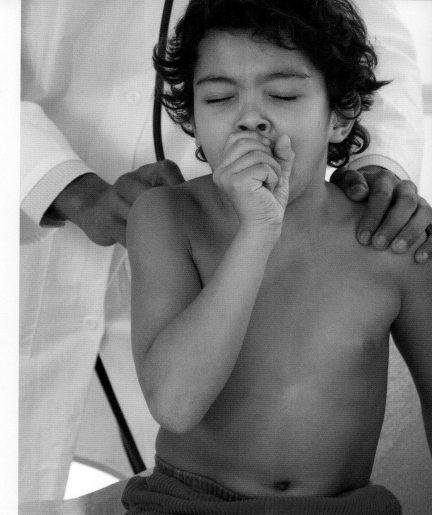

Rhinotillexomania

(rye-no-till-ex-o-may-nee-ah) A big word that simply means compulsive nose-picking! An Egyptian pharaoh even had his own personal nose picker. Most people may pick their nose several times a day, which is normal, but when you do it you can introduce bacteria from your hands into your nasal passages and cause illness.

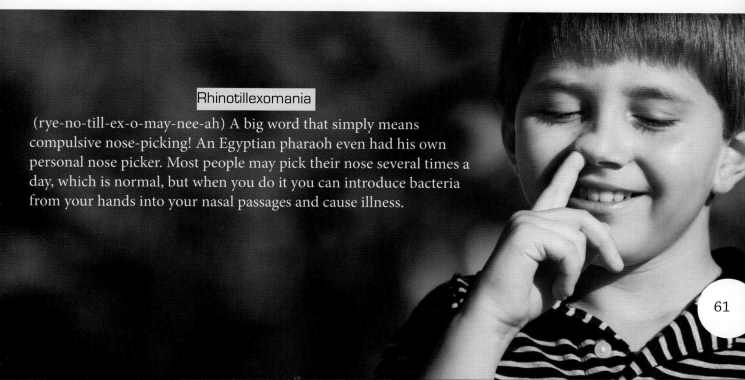

Poliomyelitis, also called polio, is a disease that affects not only the lungs but many other organ systems as well. It can lead to debilitating deformities of the legs, impairing the ability of walk. Polio is caused by a virus that invades the spinal cord and can lead to paralysis (the inability to move) of legs and the diaphragm, breathing problems, and death. A devastating epidemic occurred in the United States in 1952, over 57,000 people were afflicted with the disease.

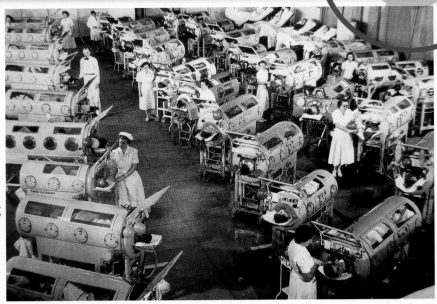
Iron lung ward filled with polio patients, Rancho Los Amigos Hospital, California (1953)

Dr. Jonas Salk and Dr. Albert Sabin are credited with bringing this horrible crippling disease under control. In 1955, Dr. Jonas Salk developed a polio vaccine. It is called the Inactivated Polio Vaccine (IPV). The inactivated polio virus is injected into a person and the body's immune system mounts a response to the virus by producing protective antibodies. These antibodies help to protect a person from contracting the disease. In 1957, Dr. Albert Sabin developed a vaccine that used a live weakened version of the polio virus that was taken by mouth. It was called the oral polio vaccine (OPV). The OPV vaccine was discontinued in the United States in 2000 because of its association with a rare serious reaction.

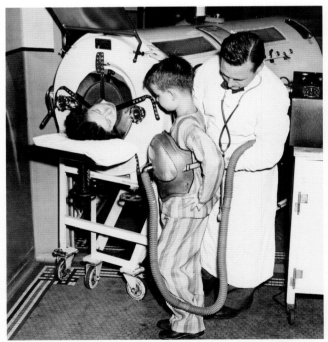
At the height of a polio epidemic, Dr. Harry Seanor, fastens the one-pound lung on an eight-year-old boy to show the difference in size to that of the 700-pound lung at left. Iron lungs were respirators to assist patients with breathing, (1949).

Dr. Jonas Salk

Dr. Albert Sabin

Paralytic Poliomyelitis

1	The poliovirus enters the body through the mouth, usually from hands contaminated with the stools of an infected person or by ingestion of contaminated food or water.
2	The poliovirus travels to the digestive tract and attaches to receptors on the intestinal walls and replicates. The poliovirus can spread from the intestinal walls into the bloodstream.
3	In 99% of cases the poliovirus causes only mild flu-like symptoms or no symptoms at all. But in 1% of cases the poliovirus spreads from the bloodstream to the central nervous system.
4	The poliovirus attacks the central nervous system, destroying nerve cells in the spinal cord.
5	The virus may destroy the nerve cells governing the muscles necessary for breathing, and the muscles in the limbs, causing paralysis, most often in the legs.
6	The poliovirus is highly contagious. Even in mild cases the poliovirus is excreted in feces that can contaminate hands, food, and water.

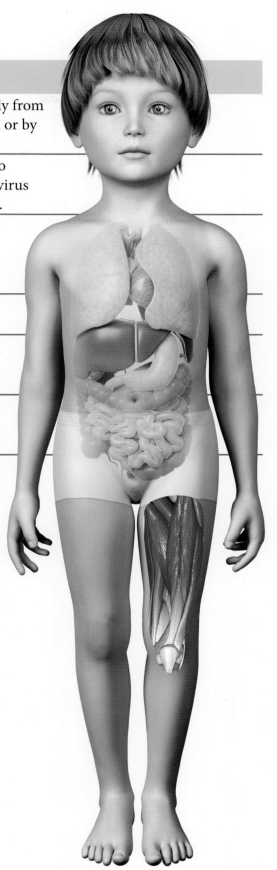

63

Franklin D. Roosevelt (FDR), the 32nd president of the United States, was one of the most famous sufferers of polio. Polio usually affected children. However, there were also adults who experienced paralysis from this virus. In 1921, FDR lost his first bid to become president of the United States. The campaign was a grueling fight. After his loss, he escaped on a family vacation to recover from the fatigue of being on the campaign trail. He was 39 years old, married with five children. He became ill while on vacation for a period of time. He recovered but never regained the full use of his legs. His legs were paralyzed. He was unable to walk. FDR kept his disability a secret when he decided on another run for the presidency. He wore braces under his pants to help support his body. He leaned into the podium or held someone's arm to support his weight. He had a special

President Franklin D. Roosevelt

wheelchair created to resemble a household chair. FDR kept his secret from the American people. He felt that if people knew he could not walk unaided it would show weakness, not only to the American people, but to the world. He was rarely photographed in his wheelchair. There are over 35,000 documented pictures of FDR; only two show him in a wheelchair.

An old proverb states that "necessity is the mother of invention." This means that only through great need are we inspired to create new things and solutions to problems. In 1938, Roosevelt, on the wings of the polio epidemic, established the National Foundation for Infantile Paralysis. Infantile paralysis was another name for polio, since children were the most affected by this disease. The purpose of the organization was to connect scientists and volunteers to assist the victims of polio as well as provide financial support for research. The National Foundation for Infantile Paralysis stills exists today. The name was changed to the March of Dimes. This name change was instituted after a nationwide campaign to raise money to fund the organization. FDR called on everyone to give whatever money they could spare. He emphasized that even amounts as small as a dime would be of great service.

"Franklin's illness... gave him strength and courage he had not had before. He had to think out the fundamentals of living and learn the greatest of all lessons — infinite patience and never ending persistence." —Eleanor Roosevelt, wife of FDR

The whirling rush of air sounds rhythmic throughout the room. Lying face up, your arms pinned to your sides and only your head peeking out of an 800-pound steel can, you try to relax as the next wave of pressure pushes the air out of your lungs.

This is a small glimpse of life in an iron lung. Though the iron lung is no longer produced, it made the difference between life and death for thousands of people during the polio epidemic in the 1950s. Today, only about 10 people worldwide still live life in the iron lung. Phillip Drinker, an engineer, and his colleagues at the Harvard School of Public Health invented a respirator that enabled paralytic polio patients to breathe. It was called the Drinker Respirator and was first introduced in 1927. It became commonly known as the "iron lung" due to its appearance.

The Drinker Respirator was very large and heavy. The magnificent thing about this life-saving technology was, it could accommodate a great range of different-sized patients. A small child to a man as large as 6 feet 4 inches and weighing up to 225 pounds could use the apparatus. Many people who required the aid of the iron lung would use it for only a few weeks until their bodies recovered from the paralysis of polio. There were others who never regained the use of their muscles or their diaphragms to assist in breathing. They were confined to the metal case for the rest of their lives.

How does it work? Great question. A person is laid on a padded cot and slid into the apparatus. The metal enclosure is snapped shut. The only thing that lies outside the container is the person's head. A soft flexible rubber collar seals the opening around their neck and the machine. There are windows along the body of the tube to allow health providers access to the patient.

A mirror is suspended over the person's head, allowing the patient a limited view of the room. A mechanical arm connected to a bellow at the foot of the chamber and was powered by an electrical motor.

Air is not actually pushed into the person's lungs. It is the pressure differences in the airtight container that allow the person to breathe. As the arm of the machine works like a piston with the bellow, it creates positive and negative pressures. When the pressure in the tube is more negative than the pressure inside the lungs, the patient's diaphragm draws down. The person inhales. When the pressure becomes more positive, higher than the pressures within the lungs, it causes the person to exhale.

Up to 100 iron lungs would run at the same time in hospital units at the peak of the polio epidemic. According to the Smithsonian Institution, the cost of an iron lung was extremely high. In the 1930s, an iron lung would cost a family a whopping $1,500. That was the going price of a house at that time. To put this in perspective, a dollar in the 1930s is equivalent to $14.25 today.

So doing the math, $1,500 in the 1930s would be over $21,000 today.

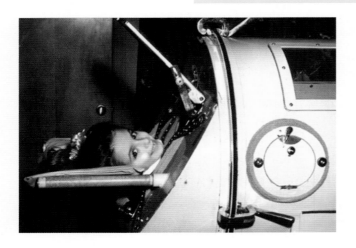

The year was 1948. On the 13th day of September, three days after her brother died from polio, 11-year-old Martha Mason began to feel ill. She became stricken with the same grave illness as her brother. Martha stayed in the hospital for a year. Finally, her parents were able to bring her home in an iron lung with assistance from the March of Dimes Foundation. It was in the iron lung that she would live the remainder of her life. Martha lived in her metallic cocoon, unable to breathe on her own, for 61 additional years.

But Martha's spirit was never paralyzed. She spread her wings and soared. With the help of multiple friends, her loving parents, and the town in which she lived. Martha was able to complete her high school studies and go on to college, graduating first in her class. During her time at Gardner Webb University she lived in the basement and communicated via intercom with her classmates and professors. She wrote for the local paper after graduation with the help of other's hands and a voice-activated computer.

As technology advanced, Martha's living situation remained the same. She stated, "By the time [alternative ways of respiration] were readily available, I had already established a lifestyle in an iron lung. After investigation and observation, I've learned that these people have [tracheotomies]; they have infections that have a lot more problems. I don't know of any one of them who has used that equipment for 60 years and had a good life with it." Mason felt her iron lung allowed her to be independent because the operation of it required no monitoring by medical professionals and allowed her to stay in her own home.

The iron lung that she lived in had a backup generator. This generator was crucial to her survival in the event of a power outage. Everyone in her town knew her. If the power went out, the fire department would immediately dispatch a crew over to her house to make sure her iron lung was functioning properly. In 2010, Martha published her memoir, *Breathe: A Lifetime in the Rhythm of an Iron Lung*. She never saw herself as a victim. Martha indeed lived a full life. She demonstrated resolve and an iron will.

Today the "iron lung" is no longer used. A special machine called a ventilator is now used to support the breathing of patients who are too sick to breathe on their own.

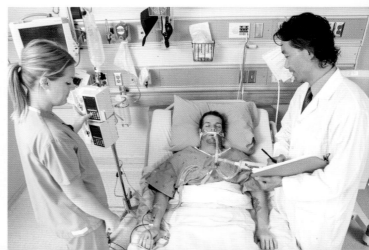

Her life got off to a rocky start. She entered this world on June 23, 1940, a sickly-premature baby, born the 20th child in a family of 22 children. At the tender age of four, this small African-American girl lost the use of her right leg due to polio. Her name was Wilma Rudolph.

Wilma's parents were told that she would never be able to walk normally. With dogged determination, they refused to accept the doctor's verdict. The Rudolphs who did their best to make a living to support their large family, knew their daughter would walk one day.

Refusing to accept no for an answer, Wilma's mother began to take Wilma for intensive therapy sessions at Meharry Hospital. It was the only facility at that time in history that would treat African Americans. Meharry was over 50 miles away from their home. Wilma went twice a week. She endured painful and grueling exercises. On Wilma's sixth birthday, she was able to walk with the assistance of leg braces, special shoes, and crutches. But her recovery did not stop there. Her mother refused to treat Wilma any differently than her siblings. By 12 years old, she was able to walk on her own. She even began to learn to run and jump.

Wilma loved to watch her siblings play and always joined in. Upon entering junior high, Wilma decided to try out for the basketball and track team. She made it! She didn't play very much, but with each passing practice she grew stronger and stronger. Her nickname became "Skeeter" because she was like a buzzing mosquito eager to get in the games. She started to excel in athletics. At a track meet at the Tuskegee Institute, Wilma ran. She lost every race she ran.

Nevertheless, Ed Temple, a coach from Tennessee State University, took notice of young Wilma. He recognized Wilma's potential and invited her to train with his collegiate track team.

Wilma ran so fast it was as if she could fly. She competed in two Olympic games, the first one at 16. In two games, she returned home with a bronze medal (third place) and three gold medals.

Franklin Delano Roosevelt, Martha Mason and Wilma Rudolph all overcame great odds to live life to the fullest. God gives us all varying talents. We all encounter varying degrees of difficulty in life. It is not what we lack but what we do with what is gifted to us.

Why does my side sometimes hurt when I run and breathe hard?

Ouch! Some people call this sharp pain you experience with heavy exercise a "side stitch." The medical term for this is called exercise-related transient abdominal pain. Don't you love it when medicine can come up with terms to describe a common phenomenon and make it sound quite complicated? This pain can be experienced when you have been running or walking vigorously. Don't worry — the pain is temporary and nothing serious. Normally, this pain is felt on the right side, not far from your belly button.

? There are many theories on the origin of this pain. Some think the exuberant movement of the legs increases the pressure in the abdomen and presses the diaphragm upward. Your respiratory rate is increased to satisfy your muscles' increased demand for oxygen, causing the lungs to press the diaphragm down. The diaphragm is then trapped in the middle, and these opposing forces give it a squeeze. The squeezing decreases the flow of blood and oxygen to the area, which leads to a sharp stabbing pain and/or cramping. Another theory is that the ligaments, special connective tissues that keep things in place, in the area of the diaphragm may experience stretching with the pounding and breathing action. To be honest, no one really knows. To be sure, the pain is real. But be assured, it won't hurt you.

Why do I hiccup?

The original term for such a reaction was "hiccough" in the early 1500s in England. The word evolved to what we now refer to as hiccups. We have onomatopoeia to thank for the name change. Onomatopoeia is simply a term for a word that is spelled and pronounced just like the sound it describes. A hiccup is produced when the diaphragm is irritated. It jerks down in a spastic manner. Air rushes into your lungs. As the air passes by your vocal cords they close suddenly and you make the well-known sound.

? This irritation can be caused by eating fast, a stomach or throat annoyance, and even becoming frightened. Typically, they only last a few minutes. The world record for hiccups is held by Charles Osborne. He had the hiccups for 69 years! Not a record that you would be interested in breaking for sure. It was said that his hiccups began in 1922 after he tried to weigh a 350-pound pig that was to be slaughtered. They did not stop until 1990. It is estimated that he hiccupped over 430 million times. At the peak of his marathon, he would hiccup up to 40 times a minute.

What causes me to sneeze when I leave a movie theater?

Achoo! I believe I've hit a snafu.

Achoo! This is no virtue.

Achoo! I can't stop, boohoo.

Cough. Sniff. I think I made a swap, yahoo.

We have all experienced that little tickle in the nose, and without any control you launch a snot rocket. This propulsion can occur due to many reasons aside from irritation. Believe it or not, some people sneeze when entering bright light after being in the dark; for example, after leaving a movie theater. This is called a photic sneeze, or a photic sneeze reflex. A reflex doesn't involve a conscious decision by the brain. You don't think about it, but your body just does it. Nearly 20 to 30 percent of all people may experience photic sneezes. So appropriately, it is also known as the ACHOO syndrome (Autosomal Dominant Compelling Helio-Ophthalmic Outburst Syndrome). It is believed to be a trait that runs in families.

The optic nerve is the nerve that connects your eyeballs to your brain. It carries signals that originate at the eye, and the brain interprets what you see. In a dark environment, your pupils dilate (become larger) to allow more light to enter your eye in the darkness. Upon exiting the theater, your optic nerve tells your pupils to constrict. This protects your eyes from the extra light. Enter another brain nerve, the trigeminal nerve. It is stimulated when your nose is irritated by something. The optic and trigeminal nerves are neighbors. They lie very close to each other. It is believed that some of the electrical impulse that runs down the optic nerve seeps over to the trigeminal nerve. This activates the trigeminal and triggers a sneeze.

Why does my nose run when I cry?

Crying produces a great deal of fluid runoff down your face. Did you know you actually have a drainage area near your eye? At the corner of your eye, you will find the lacrimal sac.

Tears flow into the sac and drain out near the tubinates in the nasal cavity. The more you cry, the more your nose runs.

Why does my nose run when it is cold?

One of the functions of your nose is to warm the air that enters it. The vessels that lie close to the nasal lining dilate (become wider) during colder conditions. This allows extra blood to flow by in order to provide additional heating power. The extra blood flow also produces extra mucus to stream out your nose.

Why is snot green?

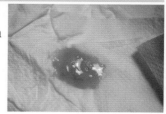

Doctors like to ask gross questions when you are sick. They may even ask you to describe the color of your snot! This certainly isn't a common topic of casual conversations. No, doctors do not have some strange interest with your body fluids. They ask this question because it may provide a clue about your illness. When you are sick, your immune system (remember when we talked about your soldiers) sends out white blood cells to fight the battle. There are several different types of white blood cells. The white blood cells that are the foot soldiers at the site of the attack are called neutrophils. The neutrophils are armed inside with special enzymes that aid in the defense. The enzyme of interest is myeloperoxidase. This enzyme contains a great deal of iron. As the fight wages, the white blood cells sacrifice themselves and spill their innards out into the mucus. Then more bacteria to fight the more brave white blood cells are called into action. The myeloperoxidase released has the characteristic green color. This spilling enzyme helps to kill the unwanted invaders. This "sick" snot is composed of dead white blood cells, discharged enzymes, and half-eaten bacteria. The longer it sits around in your sinuses, the greener it gets.

Why can fish breathe underwater and we can't?

All living animals require oxygen. Just like you, fish need oxygen. However, they satisfy their oxygen needs in a different way. The water that surrounds them is a compound of two hydrogens and one oxygen atom. Water is referred to as H_2O. This is the chemical shorthand for water's composition.

We cannot breathe the oxygen in the water because of its tight bond with hydrogen atoms. Fish "breathe" the oxygen that is dissolved in the water. (You can see an example of dissolved gases when you drink a soda pop. It fizzes when you pour it, tickling your nose. This is due to the dissolved carbon dioxide gas in it. When the gas is no longer present in the drink it becomes "flat" tasting.) Fish do not have lungs; they have gills. As they swim about, water is pushed through their gills. Interestingly, fish are cold blooded. We are warm blooded. One reason God has designed fish to be cold blooded is that it reduces their oxygen demands. The warmer you are, the more oxygen is required. Fish force water into their gills and the dissolved oxygen seeps into the walls of their blood vessels. Carbon dioxide seeps out of the vessels and is released out of the gills.

How do insects breathe?

God has created us uniquely different from the insect world. Like us, insects have the same need for oxygen in order to live. They do not have lungs like us but instead they have spiracles along the side of their exoskeletons. Spiracles are holes that allow air to enter the insect's body. The air travels down a series of tubes, and the oxygen actually dissolves into the liquid of their bodies. So insects do not technically "breathe" the way we breathe.

What causes nosebleeds?

? Remember when we were talking about the large network of blood vessels that line your nasal cavity? Because of their proximity to the surface, these vessels are particularly vulnerable. If you put your finger in your nostril, you increase your chances of producing an epistaxis (ep-i-STAK-sis). That is the smart word for nosebleed. There are other things that can cause nosebleeds. For example, a drying of the nasal passages is more common in the winter when the humidity in the air is low. Infections and allergies can also produce a nosebleed.

Why is it hard to breathe at high altitudes?

? The higher you travel above sea level, the less oxygen concentration there is in the air. The oxygen concentration at sea level is much more dense. Another way of thinking about this is that the air molecules stack upon each other and exert a greater pressure the closer you move to sea level. Physical exertion at high altitudes requires more breaths of air to obtain the normal amount of oxygen your body demands. No worries. If you stay at higher elevation for a period of time, after a few days, your body gets used to these demands by increasing the production of red blood cells. With the addition, it allows for more oxygen-carrying capabilities.

Conclusion

Psalm 139 states that we are fearfully and wonderfully made. We are part of God's creation, and with the breath that He gives let us praise Him and marvel at His creation.

Praise the LORD.
Praise God in his sanctuary;
praise him in his mighty heavens.
Praise him for his acts of power;
praise him for his surpassing greatness.
Praise him with the sounding of the trumpet,
praise him with the harp and lyre,
praise him with timbrel and dancing,
praise him with the strings and pipe,
praise him with the clash of cymbals,
praise him with resounding cymbals.
Let everything that has breath praise the LORD.
Praise the LORD!

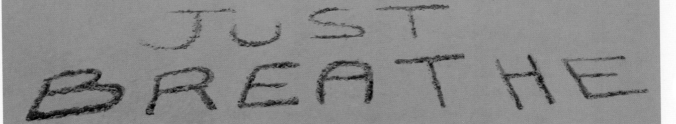

Facts: Bizarre and Gross

The desire of humans to compete in just about anything is unmatched. In Langenbruck, Germany, a competition for the longest nose in the world was held. I have no idea what type of training was required. Josef Dewold surpassed all contestants, proudly displaying his schnoz, winning the men's division with a nose measuring 4.8 inches. Margot Sikora, not to be left behind, won the women's with a 4.1-inch nose.

Medical treatments have improved over the years as our knowledge and understanding of the workings of the human body has grown. In ancient times, there were some unusual ideas of cures for diseases. Yikes!

- To cure whooping cough, ride a donkey seven times in a circle or crawl under the donkey seven times.

- To cure tuberculosis, breathe into a freshly dug hole in the ground or swallow live snails.

During the middle ages, people had no concept about the origin of infectious illnesses. They believed diseases were caused by evil vapors that permeated the skin. Bathing was not a normal practice. They thought a thick layer of sweat and dirt would keep them healthy. So they stopped bathing. In the 1500s, England's Queen Elizabeth I tried to get people to bathe more often. She felt it was a better, healthier practice. She encouraged people to take up her practice of bathing at least once a month whether they needed it or not. This was shocking and controversial. People of the time only bathed a couple of times a year.

Great or common mullein (Verbascum thapsus) has been used for almost 2,000 years as an herbal treatment for lung and skin ailments, ranging from asthma to burns. It is one of several natural herbs used for respiratory issues.

You've Got to Be Kidding

What were the little snots afraid of when they went to bed?	The Booger Man.
What is brown and sticky?	A stick.
How do you make a tissue dance?	You put a little boogie on it.
Why did the boogie cross the road?	He was getting picked on.
Knock, Knock. Who's there? Snot. Snot who?	Your joke is snot funny.
What can you keep even if you give it away?	A cold.
Why was the nose so tired?	Because he had been running all day.
When you're out with your honey, And your nose is runny, You may think it's funny,	But IT'S NOT!!! (IT SNOT)
What does a booger in love tell his girlfriend?	I am stuck on you. Or I pick you.
What do you call a skinny booger?	Slim pickings.
What is the difference between boogers and broccoli?	Kids don't eat broccoli.
Why can't your nose be 12 inches long?	Because then it would be a foot!
Doctor, how do I stop my nose from running?	Stick out your foot and trip it.
How do you prevent a summer cold?	Catch it in the winter.
Doctor: Your cough sounds better today.	Patient: It should — I practiced all night.
What did the French man say after getting caught in the rain?	Eiffel a cold coming on.
Why did the hacker give his computer a box of tissues?	Because it had a nasty virus!
What do you give a cowboy with a cold?	Cough stirrup.
You can pick your nose and you can pick your friends…	…but you can't pick your friend's nose.
Did you just pick your nose?	No, I've had it since the day I was born.
What can you catch, but not throw?	A cold.
What did the nut say when it sneezed?	Cashew!
If we breathe oxygen in the daytime, what do we breathe at night?	Nitrogen!
What do you call a dinosaur that keeps you awake at night?	A Bronto-snore-us

Word Wise!

"BOOGER" A popular term for a small mass of congealed nasal mucus.

73

❝Coughing in the theater is not a respiratory ailment. It is a criticism.❞ *Alan Jay Lerner*

❝When a man has lost all happiness, he's not alive. Call him a breathing corpse.❞ *Sophocles*

❝To be a Christian without prayer is no more possible than to be alive without breathing.❞ *Martin Luther*

❝What light is to the eyes — what air is to the lungs — what love is to the heart, liberty is to the soul of man.❞ *Robert Green Ingersoll*

❝Whenever I feel blue, I start breathing again.❞ *L. Frank Baum*

❝The longest sword, the strongest lungs, the most voices, are false measures of truth.❞ *Benjamin Whichcote*

MED+MOMENT

Careers There are a lot of different kinds of medical careers, including many focused on the respiratory system. Here are just a few:

Respiratory Therapist	Manages the airway of patients; helps in establishing an airway after a trauma, for patients in intensive care units and for sedation; gives breathing treatments; sets up and manages ventilators
Pulmonologist	A doctor who specializes in the treatment of lung conditions and disease. Education: college 4 years, medical school 4 years, internal medicine residency 3 years, pulmonary fellowship 2 to 3 years. Total training after high school is 14 to 15 years.
Cardiopulmonary Lab Specialist	Helps patient understand and manage health problems, works with patients with diseases such as emphysema, heart attack, asthma, and Chronic Obstructive Pulmonary Disease (COPD)
Pulmonary Lab Tech	Conducts pulmonary function testing
Pulmonology	Medical specialty that deals with the study and treatment of diseases involving the respiratory tract

"A large nose is the mark of a witty, courteous, affable, generous, and liberal man." *Cyrano de Bergerac*

"The air is the only place free from prejudice." *Bessie Coleman*

"A nation that destroys its soils destroys itself. Forests are the lungs of our land, purifying the air and giving fresh strength to our people." *Franklin D. Roosevelt*

"The highlight of my childhood was making my brother laugh so hard that food came out of his nose." *Garrison Keillor*

"A smile is happiness you'll find right under your nose."

Tom Wilson

75

Alton, Steve. *Blood and Goo and Boogers Too! A Heart-Pounding Pop-up Guide to the Circulatory and Respiratory Systems.* New York: Dial Books, 2008.

Barnhill, Kelly Regan. *Sick, Nasty Medical Practices.* Mankato, MN: Capstone Press, 2009.

Beccia, Carlyn. *I Feel Better with a Frog in My Throat.* New York: Harcourt Publishing Company, 2010.

Becker, Christine. *Gross Anatomy.* Toronto, Canada: RGA Publishing Group, Inc., 1996.

Branzei, Sylvia. *Really Gross Things About Your Body.* New York, NY: Penguin Putnam, 2002.

Conley, Kate A. *Joseph Priestley and the Discovery of Oxygen,* Hockessin, DE: Mitchell Lane Publishers, 2006.

Cunningham, Kevin. *Disease in History: Flu.* Greensboro, NC: Morgan Reynolds Publishing, Inc., 2009.

Cunningham, Kevin. *Pandemics.* New York, NY: Scholastic Inc., 2012.

Dawson, Ian. *The History of Medicine, Prehistoric and Egyptian Medicine,* New York, NY: Enchanted Lion Books, 2005.

Dendy, Leslie, and Mel Boring. *Guinea Pig Scientists: Bold Self-Experimenters in Science and Medicine.* New York, NY: Henry Holt and Company, 2005.

Dowswell, Paul. *Medicine.* Chicago, IL: Reed Educational and Professional Publishing, 2002.

Eldon, Dorry. *Lyrical Life Science: Volume 3 — The Human Body,* Corvallis, OR: Lyrical Learning, 1998.

Emery, Joanna. *Gross and Disgusting Things About the Human Body.* Canada: Blue Bike Books, 2007.

Fleming, Deena. *More Gross Jokes.* New York, NY: Tangerine Press, 2005.

Getz, David. *Purple Death: The Mysterious Flu of 1918.* New York, NY: Henry Holt and Company, 2000.

Helleman, A., and Bryan H. Bunch. *The Timetables of Science: A Chronology of the Most Important People and Events in the History of Science.* New York: Simon and Schuster, 1991.

Herlihy, Barbara L., and Nancy K. Maebius. *The Human Body in Health and Illness.* Philadelphia, PA: W.B. Saunders, 2000.

Johnson, Jinny. *Under the Microscope. Breathing — How We Use Air.* Danbury, CT: Grolier, Inc. 1988.

Kalman, Bobbie. *Early Health and Medicine.* New York: Crabtree Publishing Company, 1991.

Lambert, Mark. *How Our Bodies Work: The Lungs and Breathing.* Englewood, NJ: Schoolhouse Press, Inc., 1988.

Larsen, C.S. *Crust and Spray: Gross Stuff in Your Eyes, Ears, Nose, and Throat.* Gross Body Science. Minneapolis, MN: Millbrook Press, 2010.

Llamas, Andreu. *Respiration and Circulation.* Milwaukee, WI: Gareth Stevens Publishing, 1988.

Masoff, Joy. *Oh, Yuck! The Encyclopedia of Everything Nasty.* New York, NY: Workman Publishing Company, 2000.

Mason, Estate of Martha. *Breath: A Lifetime in the Rhythm of an Iron Lung: A Memoir.* New York: First Bloomsbury USA, 2010.

Miller, Connie Colwell. *The Snotty Book of Snot.* Mankato, MN: Capstone Press, 2010.

Murphy, Glenn. *Why Is Snot Green? And Other Extremely Important Questions (and Answers).* New York: Scholastic, 2007.

Orr, Tamra. *Avian Flu.* New York, NY: The Rosen Publishing Group, Inc., 2007.

Perl, Lila. *Don't Sing Before Breakfast, Don't Sleep in the Moonlight: Everyday Superstitions and How They Began.* New York, NY: Clarion Books, 1988.

Petechuk, David. *The Respiratory System.* Westport, CT: Greenwood Press, 2004.

Peters, Stephanie True. *The Battle Against Polio.* Tarrytown, NY: Benchmark Books, 2005.

Peters, Stephanie True. *The 1918 Influenza Pandemic.* Tarrytown, NY: Benchmark Books, 2005.

Platt, Richard. *Plagues, Pox and Pestilence.* New York, NY: Kingfisher, 2011.

Rooney, Anne. *The Story of Medicine.* London: Arcturus Publishing Limited, 2009.

Rosaler, Maxine. *Cystic Fibrosis.* New York, NY: The Rosen Publishing Group, Inc., 2007.

Sadler, Thomas W. *Langman's Medical Embryology,* Philadelphia, PA: Lippincott Williams and Wilkins, 2011.

Stewart, Melissa. *Up Your Nose! The Secrets of Schnozes and Snouts.* The Gross and Goofy Body. New York: Marshall Cavendish, 2009.

Stille, Darlene R. *Extraordinary Women of Medicine.* Danbury, CT: Children's Press, Grolier Publishing, 1997.

Stimola, Aubrey. *Ebola.* New York, NY: The Rosen Publishing Group, Inc., 2011.

Szpirglas, Jeff. *Gross Universe: Your Guide to All Disgusting Things Under the Sun.* Toronto, Canada: Maple Tree Press, Inc., 2004.

Weitzman, I., Eva Blank, Alison Benjamin, and Rosanne Green. *Jokelopedia: The Biggest, Best, Silliest, Dumbest Joke Book Ever.* New York, NY: Workman Publishing Company, Inc., 2000.

Websites:

Mythbusters, TV show, Episode: Snot Meter, http://www.discovery.com/tv-shows/mythbusters/videos/snot-meter.htm

www.pbs.org/wnet/nature/episodes/underdogs/the-bloodhounds-amazing-sense-of-smell/350/

The Great White Plague: The Culture of Death and the Tuberculosis Sanatorium by: Richard Sucre, http://www.faculty.virginia.edu/blueridgesanatorium/death.htm

http://www.washingtontimes.com/news/2014/aug/24/north-texan-one-of-10-still-living-in-iron-lung/?page=all

http://www.brainyquote.com

http://www.culinarylore.com/food-history:origin-of-the-name-of-the-adams-apple

INDEX

78

Photo credits: